FOREWORD BY ROGER STAUBACH

RUN TO THE FIRE

THE TRUE STORY OF RICK COLLINS

AS TOLD BY CHAD COLLINS

FREILING
PUBLISHING

Written by Christen M. Jeschke

Published by Freiling Publishing,
a division of Freiling Agency, LLC.

P.O. Box 1264
Warrenton, VA 20188

www.FreilingPublishing.com

PB ISBN: 978-1-956267-81-5
HB ISBN: 978-1-956267-86-0
eBook ISBN: 978-1-956267-82-2

Printed in the United States of America

Dedication

This book is dedicated to:

- Linda Collins
- Caryn, Matt, and Lucas Moore
- Kelly, Carson, Chief, and Caroline Collins
- Veterans of the US Armed Services, past and present, and their families
- The Fitzgerald, Shubert, Burkett, Johnson, Bozeman, Spencer, and Beagle Families
- Family and Many Friends of Rick Collins
- Players and those who coached with Rick Collins

Contents

Foreword

As a fellow Vietnam Veteran, I have the highest respect for those like Rick Collins who left parts of themselves physically and emotionally in Southeast Asia. While I was known for having nicknames like "Roger the Dodger" and "Captain Comeback," I have the highest admiration for heroes who have left it all on the field of life. Rick's trials and tribulations resulting in life and limb-altering service in the Vietnam War alone would leave you in deep respect just like it does for me. I had a chance to meet Rick Collins when he was recovering in the VA hospital in 1970 in Dallas. I was starting a career using my healthy legs and arms in the National Football League, and Rick was struggling to take his first steps after losing the use of his. Little did I know then that I would be the honored person to write the foreword of a book outlining the life this young amputee soldier would live. During that period, our heroic soldiers didn't receive the welcome they deserved, and sadly some didn't recover in more ways than one.

Knowing the life story and legacy that Rick Collins lived out creates a sense of pride and respect for how that young soldier I met in the early days of his journey in the VA Hospital chose to live out his life. I have always believed in competing with every ounce of everything I have in every aspect of my own life. Rick Collins' life lessons are a playbook for all of us to carefully study relative to our own lives or those we are trying to support in their perseverance journey. In this book, you will see firsthand what it means to live a full life on the two-yard line. My hope for you is that whether on offense or defense, while facing down the challenges of what is ahead of you, you choose to live a life of "Running to the Fire" like you will see Rick Collins do throughout this mesmerizing book. We need more stories of inspiration like Rick Collins' life.

—Roger Staubach
Vietnam Veteran and NFL Hall of Fame

You've never lived until you have almost died. For those who have fought for it, life has a flavor the protected will never know.

—Unknown

Introduction

Run to the fire.

Run to the fire.

At some point in our lives, particularly when we're children, we all think our dad is a superhero. Even without the mask and cape, Dad is faster than a speeding bullet, more powerful than a locomotive, able to leap tall buildings in a single bound, and even able to run into a ball of fire.

That was one of my first memories of my dad—running into a blaze. I was just a little boy, but I still remember the horror and the heroism of watching my dad run toward and disappear into a giant ball of orange and yellow flames. It takes a true hero to run toward danger and not flee from it. My dad was just this type of man.

Rick Collins didn't look like a superhero. His body had been wrecked by a war far away and a major car accident at home. Disabled and racked with intense daily pain, Rick Collins was not a likely superhero. However, this is exactly who my father was—he was a hero who would run to the fire when challenged. The memories both haunt me and make me swell with pride.

It was a hot, dark, peaceful night, and our family sedan traversed forgotten rural roads listening to my dad's favorite '50s and '60s rock-n-roll. A country road can be a desolate place—a barren blackness lit only by starlight and the dim glow drifting from the headlights of a passing car. It was later in the evening, around 10:00 p.m., and most children were already home, tucked into their beds for the night, while we weaved around the potholes, doggedly making our way home after visiting relatives in town.

My dad was driving, his strong hands mechanically operating the vehicle's foot pedals, as what remained of his disabled legs lay motionless, unable to assist him. One leg had been sacrificed through amputation in service to the Vietnam War; the mangled remains of the other leg had been preserved, only to be shattered in a vehicle accident less than a year later. He fought every day to live a full and active life despite what others saw as extremely limiting disabilities, and this included driving the family car.

My sister and I were sleepy, and as such, we were uncharacteristically quiet. I sat quietly between my parents while my little sister, Caryn, lay sleeping in the backseat. I remember staring silently up at the moon, mesmerized by the dark expanse surrounding us. My mom and dad engaged in conversation while listening to those oldies but goodies on the radio, interspersed with lapses of contented silence as the car gained mile after mile.

Suddenly ahead, the sky erupted in a flash of light! The road turned to reveal an inferno of flames licking at a lone vehicle at a T-crossing ahead. Our calm night was jarringly interrupted by the jolting flash of a fire engulfing a car as thick waves of black smoke disappeared into the inky darkness of the night sky above. I had never seen such a sight.

My dad threw the car into park, and not losing a second, he sprung into immediate action. There was no pause, no hesitancy, and no hitch in his movements as he determined what to do. He was a blur of frenetic motion propelled forward. He yelled to my mom to go for help at a nearby house. Before she managed to wrestle my sister and me out of the car, my dad took off toward the fire. His gait was the labored and jaunty jog of a man who had been told he would never walk again, yet managed to do so with a prosthesis and great persistence. My dad wouldn't allow anything to stop him from his mission.

My five-year-old brain could barely process my fears. Why would my dad run to the fire? My dad was going to die. "Daddy!" I screamed hysterically as my mom hauled my two-year-old sister and me off to get help.

"Daddy!" I sobbed, my heart nearly bursting with relief when we returned to the scene. I was certain that the burning blaze would swallow him—my superhero.

When we found my dad, he was gasping for breath, and his clothes and hair were singed with smoke. Miraculously, he successfully dragged a teenage girl nearly half a football field from her burning vehicle. Paramedics and firefighters soon swarmed to the site, tending to the teenage girl and extinguishing the fire. She was rushed to the hospital, and we would later discover that my dad had indeed saved her young life.

She was pinned between the steering wheel and the collapsed seat; the rescue crew would explain that somehow in an incredible feat of strength, my dad had forcefully broken the steering column to save this girl from certain death. They looked rather stunned at the image of my dad's broken body tearing through a burning car like a bear.

There's no doubt that God was at work that night, supernaturally giving my dad life-saving strength. My dad's motivation to run to the fire was most likely made bolder by his own devastating loss: years earlier, he had lost his former wife, Linda, and first son, Ricky Lynn, in a tragic and catastrophic automobile accident that had also claimed his mother-in-law, Joyce Mayhall. Maybe the haunting visions of their deaths moved him into action, but the fact is that very few people would have reacted with the strength and courage that he showed. He didn't hesitate for even a moment. He didn't stop to consider his safety, pain, or limitations.

This incident would be a moment seared into my memory forever. This action personified my dad—he shattered all limiting expectations for himself in the heroic pursuit of a valuable life. Selflessly saving this teenage girl, he humbly and unassumingly left the scene without giving his name. What Rick Collins left that night was far greater: he left a legacy written on the hearts and minds of those who carry his memories.

From these memories, I have gleaned the most valuable lessons that are far too important to be preserved only in family lore and legacy. Rick Collins' life unfolded much like a movie filled with dramatic trials, tragedy, and highs contrasted with unimaginable lows. Yet, these devastating circumstances birthed a quiet faithfulness that shone every day, and within the seemingly inane moments of daily intention, the most incredible life lessons emerged.

What you're holding and reading now is not a memoir. Yes, I'm going to tell you some stories you won't soon forget. But more importantly, I'm going to share with you the lessons I learned—that we *all* learned—through my dad's life. Some are lessons you already know but don't often practice. After reading this book, I hope you'll be motivated to make that practice permanent. Other lessons you might understand for the first time. Rick truly led a profound life and left us with some profound lessons. This is not a book about disability, although he was disabled. This is not a book about surviving trauma, although he did. This is also not merely a collection of stories, although the stories are memorable! This is a book about endurance. You'll learn about lessons of love, perseverance, faith, steadfastness, and gratefulness—things we all know and hear about but often fail to live.

You'll also learn a few things about Texas and the football gridiron, two places my dad loved and where he spent most of his life. You learn more about character on the two-yard line than anywhere else in life. Rick couldn't run up the middle while carrying the ball, but as a coach, he did what few could do. Coaches who can outline plays on a blackboard are a dime a dozen. The coaches who win are the ones who can teach and motivate their players. Winning isn't everything, but the will to win is everything.

I pray that this book will positively influence, challenge, and inspire your journey through life. You might never face a real fire, but we all have our own fires. Join my dad and me as we share with you where and how to find the grit to run directly to it. May the lessons that you learn transform you into the kind of hero that, when met with inevitable obstacles or indescribably difficult challenges, runs to the fire.

CHAPTER 1

Know Who You Are

His character was created with intention in the day-to-day battles to do right and live a life of love that impacted everyone he met.

When we were born, we carried with us the legacy and lineage of our parents, our grandparents, and all of our ancestors. This is where we first find our identity; it's what our minds tell us about ourselves.

Our storyline is birthed with the memories, expectations, thoughts, and actions of the people we were born to—our family. Family is where we get our sense of self; if we don't have this sense, life can be a wandering and aimless journey. Sometimes there's a missing piece of the puzzle. Identity can become a lifelong struggle, whether you are adopted or from a "broken" home. Putting it all together isn't always easy when you don't know where you came from.

What is your storyline? How did it all begin? Are you still searching for your identity? If so, there's so much you can learn from my dad, Rick Collins.

Rick Collins wasn't born with a strong sense of identity and self because he was abandoned by his father at birth. But despite this missing piece, he still grew up to be uniquely self-confident, brave, and determined. How so? It all started in his kindergarten class.

The streets of Dallas, Texas, hummed with excitement as the sweltering summer sun beat down on excited families preparing for their first day of school.

Children calling, dogs barking, and groups of students gathering at the bus stop with lunch pails in hand signaled the start of a new school year. "Ricky" was one of these children as he eagerly anticipated his kindergarten debut.

"Ricky! "Ricky!" His neighborhood friends affectionately called out his childhood nickname as he ran to join them.

Some children walked to school while others piled on to beat-up school buses that meandered through their routes, gathering kids at every stop. Dressed in their best first-day-of-school clothes, children jarred and jolted with each shake and turn of the bus, laughing and giggling as they waved goodbye to nervous parents. Spit-shined shoes and hand-me-down clothes were the neighborhood norm, and Rick blended right in.

His elementary school was situated in a lower economic area of Dallas. Rick's teacher warmly welcomed the class on his first day of kindergarten. "It is so nice to have all of you in my kindergarten class this year; please raise your hand when I call your name," said the teacher, a friendly smile gracing her face. Rick sat up straight in his seat, waiting for his name to be called. He was alert and eager to belong to this class. The teacher began going through the roll alphabetically.

"Edith Adams." A small girl raised her hand eagerly. "That's me!"

"Thomas Becker." A hand shot up so quickly that its force almost pulled the owner of that hand from his seat.

"Richard Collins," the teacher read through the roll. No one answered. "Richard Collins," the teacher said again, looking out at the class. My dad didn't move. The other kids began to squirm, uncomfortable in the ensuing silence.

This teacher's eyes rose pointedly above her reading glasses as she stared down her nose directly at my dad. "Richard Collins?" she said in both a question and an accusatory tone.

My dad shifted slightly in his seat before meeting her gaze and matching her stare for stare. "My name is Ricky Fitzgerald."

He spoke with direct confidence and assurance far beyond his age. After all, he knew without a doubt that he was a Fitzgerald. His mom was a Fitzgerald. His grandparents, aunts, uncles, and cousins were all Fitzgeralds. So, of course, that is who he was. He was a Fitzgerald—except that he wasn't. He was Richard Collins. My dad didn't even know his own name, his real identity.

The lone Collins in a family of Fitzgeralds, Ricky had no idea that he was anything but a Fitzgerald.

Rick's mother, Ruth Fitzgerald, was only fourteen when she became pregnant with him. Rick's biological father abandoned them both. The only thing aside from life that Frank Collins left his son was the last name, Collins. This is the same last name that I now bear as well.

But Rick had been raised a Fitzgerald. Cared for by his mom and hardworking grandparents, he fought to survive as a young boy born into a humble working family. Various Fitzgerald relatives pitched in, keeping an eye out for him and ensuring that boisterous swarms of family members always surrounded him. It was Fitzgeralds who watched him and guided him. It was the Fitzgeralds who raised him and shared family dinners with him.

Hearing his teacher say, "Richard Collins" in reference to him sounded unfamiliar. It was as if she were talking to someone he had not yet met. He wasn't sure that it fit who he knew himself to be. But it did not matter. He'd already developed a strong sense of worth in the family who raised him, not the man who abandoned him.

This was a defining moment for him. It shook him to discover that he may not be a Fitzgerald after all. As the other kids in his class taunted him and mocked him for not knowing his name or family, he chose to fight to forge his path. Rick Collins would be a boy determined to create his own legacy. The kids could tease all they wanted to. He had Fitzgerald fight combined with his own brand of Collins tenacity. It didn't matter who or what he knew or didn't know about his father's family. He chose to build his life around those who knew and loved him.

His identity wasn't what he thought it was, but he would make a new identity. He would carve out a future for Rick Collins that would instill identity and legacy in his family for years to come.

He did just that.

Rick Collins became a little piece of all the people he loved. His mother's perseverance molded his boldness in the face of insurmountable odds, raising him even as she grew herself from a naïve teen into a capable, confident, Christian woman. She gave him her faith, too, praying for him every day, taking him to church, and teaching him that God had a purpose for his life that was greater than he was.

His persistence and hard work to provide for his family were borrowed from his grandparents, who took care of their family's needs while helping raise him. His grandfather, the Fitzgerald family's diligent patriarch, cared for Ricky as if he were one of his sons. He worked tirelessly and often picked up extra income by working at the mill or running trucks full of fruits and vegetables to and from the Dallas Farmers' Market.

From his uncles, Gene, Marvin, Walter, and Tom, Rick gleaned a love of country and family. They all had served in World War II and had the shrapnel to show for it. He loved listening to their vivid lore-filled war stories and marveled at their heroism. His uncles Gene and Marvin helped raise him alongside their sons, Ronnie, Bobby, Steve, and Mark. Ricky was one of the pack, along with his other cousins Chris and Randy Burkett. From this bond, he learned loyalty, love, and the foundations of fighting for what is important. There wasn't anything that their little band wouldn't have done for each other, and they continued in this loyal and protective course throughout their lives. This was Rick's identity.

Rick would continue to shape his identity from the people he surrounded himself with, taking their strengths and learning to bolster his own. His path would be different, but he would craft his identity from the foundations of family.

Eventually, Rick's mom would marry Robert Shubert. He was blue-collar and hardworking like my dad's uncles. He treated Ruth respectfully and was a steadying example for ornery teenage Rick. Robert taught Rick to treat people with respect, to honor commitments, and most importantly, not to shy away from a good old-fashioned fight if the circumstances called for it.

These characteristics continued to mold my dad as he became the Rick Collins I knew—a man whose identity went far beyond a name. His character was created with intention in the day-to-day battles to do right and live a life of love that impacted everyone he met. His identity built on the strength of the family foundations he knew, Rick Collins blazed a path that few could ever follow.

CHAPTER 2

Don't Fear the Fight

***When confronted by evil, he was the first to
plant his feet and put his fists in the air.***

Football coaching great Tom Landry once said, "People striving, being knocked down and coming back, this is what builds character in a man." And he'd know, right? My dad was knocked down so many times, and from such a young age, it's no wonder he took on the character of a "fighter." But he didn't look for a fight. He simply understood what it means to fight for yourself, for your beliefs and values, and for others who needed a wingman. When confronted by evil, he was the first to plant his feet and put his fists in the air. Sometimes he'd lose, and sometimes he'd win. But defeat was never permanent. Rick taught us that as long as you remain willing to get up and try again, there's no stopping you from reaching your goals. If you want something badly enough, realize that your tenacity can get you to where you are headed. Sometimes half the struggle is just hanging in there until the miracle happens. Whatever your struggles, you can decide that no matter how tough it gets, even if life knocks you down, you'll get back up again and never stop fighting. Everyone knew this about Ricky, but no one more than his family.

My dad had two younger sisters, Tammy and Brenda, and a younger brother Rocky whom he adored. He was their protector, and they teasingly said that his fists were registered as deadly weapons at the Mesquite and Dallas Police Departments! The truth is that although they were not registered as deadly weapons, his fighting fists often garnered him unwanted visits to principal offices and these police stations, where he had to explain the reasons for his defense. And in fact, he was never indicted, jailed, or accused of an unfair right. Ricky fought for his family, he fought fiercely on the football field, and when his country needed him, he fought, nearly to his death, in Vietnam.

Born on September 6, 1949, Rick faced challenges from birth. Practically a child herself, Rick's mom hardly even knew of the World War that had just ended. Texas, the world Ricky was born into, was fast-changing. Before the war, Texas was sparsely populated; there were more people living in New York City than in the entire state of Texas. Teen parenthood was scorned and shamed, but Ruth valiantly raised her son with the support of her parents and a nearby network of extended family.

If there were no family members to keep an eye on him, Rick would play on the street with the other neighborhood kids. The Dallas streets were tough, but the kids would gather for ball games or other neighborhood camaraderie. Dallas was urban and had a bustling community. Each community watched out for its own—especially family. This taught my dad about loyalty; once you became his friend, he had your back. He brimmed with confidence because he knew that no matter what the world threw at him, someone would be there at his side, fighting for him. And if someone messed with one of his group, he did not hesitate to defend him with his bare fists. This is what close friends and family do for you, and it's why, even today, we cherish family. Family is where the foundation is built, then and now.

The Fitzgeralds had scrapped and scraped to establish themselves in the poorer side of town, but Rick didn't let the lack of resources define him; his fight was a battle of wills to work hard and make a future for his family. Ricky learned from this and applied it as well.

With Fitzgerald relatives spread throughout the city of Dallas, Texas, my dad was often left in the care of whatever family members could watch him, constantly roaming the streets with his cousins and friends. He quickly learned that even for a child, the streets were tough, and he had to be fast with his fists if someone needed protection. His Fitzgerald and Burkett cousins were his blood, but more importantly, they became like brothers. And no one messed with his family or friends if Ricky was around.

By age five, my dad was tasked with accompanying a relative or two to downtown bars and night spots.

With no one else to watch him, he would tag along, entertained by the drinking, hustle, and sound of the developing city of Dallas. The rough crowds in these places sharpened him with a toughness not meant for someone his age as he fought for self-preservation and to protect anyone threatening his family. As he grew, he gained a notorious reputation. He was infamous—not for starting fights, but for finishing them.

When he was in middle school, his stepdad moved their family from Hondo Street near downtown Dallas to the working-class suburb of Mesquite. At school, his new classmates quickly learned that no one messed with Ricky. They recognized that he was "that guy." He wasn't a bully but was also not someone you challenged. By nature, he was a protector. Loyal and loving to his friends, he was not afraid to fight on their behalf if anyone hurt or threatened them. He established his reputation for toughness, and the other school kids kept a respectful distance. While Dad didn't go looking for fights, he wasn't afraid to fight for what mattered.

Rick was incredibly likable yet also ornery. His teachers delighted in his vibrant personality but hated his propensity for truancy, mischief, and fistfights. The teachers, school administrators, and coaches at Mesquite ISD all saw potential in him that needed to be channeled in the right direction. If Rick's adventurous and fighting spirit weren't guided, it would ruin him. Recognizing this, they pushed him toward the natural discipline provided within athletics.

He played baseball and enjoyed it, but his real passion for sports grew on the gridiron. Football was the sport that captured his fierce and feisty spirit and honed it. He played linebacker and running back—two positions that require a thirst for competitive contact-filled violence. He lived for this game. They say that football doesn't build character; it eliminates the weak ones. Well, there was no eliminating Rick. Practice after practice, game after game, he grew a reputation for being a brute force on the field.

Lacing up his cleats, putting on his pads, and going head to head with all the force that fueled him was a sheer delight to my dad. He lost teeth, broke bones, and kept coming back for more. His coaches marveled at his toughness and agility. He would fight and get knocked down, spit out a mouthful of blood, smile, and go back for more. Football is strange that way—a violent ballet on a grass-paved stage. It is grit, fight, and determination; it is also getting knocked down repeatedly, yet rising to return, overcome, and gain the win in the end.

Corralling my dad's fiercely independent and adventurous streak was a battle in itself, one fight that football helped shape. Football helped guide him, but my dad held an intrinsic fighting spirit deeply ingrained in his nature.

His friend Rocky Johnson would recollect, "I got to know Rick when we were around twelve to thirteen years old. Rick was a tough kid, and he ran with a tough crowd through our teen years. He was NOT mean or a bully, but I will say he was the guy you wanted on your team when the fight breaks out. I believe that toughness served him well later in his life. He and I became even closer when we became brothers-in-law. I was twenty years old when Rick came back from 'Nam. I'm sure that everyone has had what they would consider a life-altering experience in their lifetime, maybe more than one. I lost track of those experiences in Rick's life. That's where this toughness I alluded to comes into play. Whenever you are out with a group of guys and you start talking about the fastest man you've ever seen or the guy who jumps the highest and the conversation goes on and inevitably comes around to the strongest guy you know of, I've got them all beat when I say, 'Take a seat; let me tell you about this guy I know.' I believe everyone on earth was put here for a reason, a purpose, if you will. God does not make mistakes, and He knew that somewhere along the way, we would need that strong man, that hero, and He said, 'Hey, I've got the man right here; his name is Rick Collins.'"

My dad never feared the fight. He fought until he got tackled, and then he bounced back up for the next hike. He rallied and regrouped, and his teammates rallied and regrouped around him. Nothing could keep Rick down. This was his nature. This was who my dad was each day, in every challenge.

.

CHAPTER 3

A Sacrifice As Big As Texas

*If there was a need to fight, serve, or protect,
he ran to the challenge.*

Any proud Texan will tell you with a distinctive Southern drawl that "Everything's bigger and better in Texas." Texas' pride in its vast state is represented in the big hair, big hats, and big hearts of its citizens. This state pride is matched only by the love of two things: the United States of America and a fierce passion and devotion to football.

In 1959, when Rick was ten years old, Texas got its first AFL professional football team, the Houston Oilers. The following year, in 1960, they added an NFL team to the mix: the Dallas Cowboys. Texans were fed football, growing up on the gridiron and dreaming of basking in the glow of the Friday night lights.

My dad relished the Friday night football games as he sought to make his mark in the same stadiums filled with the raucous cries of boisterous fans. The whole city seemed to shut down as a sea of rowdy onlookers flowed into the packed stadiums. Wooden bleachers bowed under the weight of the fans worshipping at the idol of football.

The crowds chanted, yelling and booing as if one body of pulsing energy that rhythmically gyrated in response to each successful rush or winning play. This was what Texas was all about—a fierce pride and fight that matched Rick's own fervor.

The only thing Rick loved more than the lights, the field, and the fray of the game was the beautiful Linda Faye Mayhall. Pretty and intelligent, Linda was a shining light that caught his eye and held him captive. Linda would cheer him on from her seat on the splintering pine bleachers, her encouraging voice lost in the echoes of others shouting their team onto victory. Sometimes Linda's sister, Jackie, would join her, mooning over Rick's pal Rocky Johnson. Even then, both sisters knew that they had found true love in the hallways of high school. Rocky was Jackie's beau, and Ricky was Linda's; the four would form an enduring friendship.

The celebrations on football fields throughout Texas contrasted starkly with what was going on elsewhere in the world. Born on the heels of World War II and the cusp of the Korean War, Rick didn't take for granted the cost of freedom. By the time his sixteenth birthday came around, America was already embroiled in another ominous battle that would claim the lives of thousands of Americans and Vietnamese.

As Russia and the United States remained locked in a tense Cold War standoff, tensions escalated between communist North Vietnam and American allies in South Vietnam. In March of 1965, U.S. Marines landed on the beaches of their South Vietnam allies, officially entering into a bloody, broiling conflict with communist North Vietnam.

Americans were war-weary, having lost generations of sons and daughters to continuing conflicts. The Korean War had taken over a thousand Texan boys, and World War II had taken the lives of over 22,000 Texas soldiers who sacrificed their last breaths for the security of freedom. Thirty-three Texans had been awarded the Medal of Honor in the Second World War, and Texas boasted the most highly decorated American from that war, Lieutenant Audie L. Murphy.

Enlisting in the war in Greenville, Texas, Murphy would receive the Medal of Honor and every award for valor that the United States gave. Murphy would famously comment, "The true meaning of America, you ask? It's in a Texas rodeo, in a policeman's badge, in the sound of laughing children, in a political rally, in a newspaper. . . . In all these things, and many more, you'll find America. In all these things, you'll find freedom. And freedom is what America means to the world. And to me." Texans lived their larger-than-life freedom in all the traditions and celebrations their grand state had to offer.

Rick Collins was a son of Texas, which meant that as much as he liked the freedom of the fight on the football field, he also felt a vital duty to protect it. The fabric of freedom that wove through the Texas flag and state traditions wrapped around Rick, instilling in him a growing sense of duty to a call much greater than himself.

The Vietnam War was boiling, and as casualty numbers continued to climb, protests against the war began to mount, starting on college campuses and quickly making their way across America. The draft brought the war to the home front as more than 2.2 million young men were conscripted to fight in a war that many did not believe in. Baby-faced boys, often barely out of high school, were torn from their families and sent to boot camps where they would be shined up and shipped out to foreign jungles far from home.

Like Rick Collins, many of these boys had grown up idolizing the war stories of their heroes—their grandfathers, fathers, and uncles who had served in the hopes that the next generation wouldn't have to, yet that is precisely what they were being called to do. Mothers were asked to give up their sons, yet these same women lived within the tortured trauma of what their husbands or fathers carried back from their own brutal service. Those that returned were often a shadow of the men they knew before as haunted ghosts of death and violence plagued their dreams and tortured their waking memories.

The increasing intensity of protestors matched families' hesitancy to sacrifice their sons as violent acts erupted and dissenters' voices clamored to be heard. Norman Morrison, a thirty-one-year-old protestor, was so overcome by the lives being lost to the war that he lit himself on fire in front of the Pentagon, just forty feet below the Secretary of Defense Robert S. McNamara's third-floor window. Horrified onlookers ripped Morrison's infant daughter from his arms as he erupted in a pillar of kerosene-fueled fire.

McNamara would later recall the incident: "At twilight that day, a young Quaker named Norman R. Morrison, father of three . . . burned himself to death within forty feet of my Pentagon window. . . . Morrison's death was a tragedy not only for his family but also for me and the country. It was an outcry against the killing that was destroying the lives of so many Vietnamese and American youth."

My dad weighed his thoughts about the war while he worked his way through high school and got engaged to his sweetheart, Linda. Like many young men of the 1960s, Rick watched the news coming out of Vietnam with rapt attention. Education beyond high school wasn't a priority for Rick as generations of his family had worked hard and planned well to make ends meet without a college education, so he focused on doing the same. Rick married Linda in high school, and with his first focus on what was soon to be a burgeoning family, Rick decided to quit high school and enlist in the U.S. Army. He thought that the Army would be a good career path to help him provide for his family, but later, he would acknowledge that he recognized a need for the Army to bring him discipline, a life career plan, and a pathway to change his life in a positive way. Enlisting in the Army as an eighteen-year-old in 1968, when so many were trying to avoid it, was an uncommon choice, but my dad felt that he had a duty and jumped to the front of the line.

Running into the firefight that was the violence in Vietnam was not something uncharacteristic for Rick Collins. If there was a need to fight, serve, or protect, he ran to the challenge. Rick didn't want to be drafted. He wanted to volunteer on his own big-hearted Texan terms. He later modestly recalled, "It was just what I had to do."

CHAPTER 4

Facing Fear

His faith would carry him when all else crumbled.

My dad described basic training at Fort Polk, Louisiana, as what he considered "the worst place on earth at the time." Fort Polk was renowned as the "Home of the Combat Infantryman," and thousands of young men began their army experience with basic training and advanced infantry training there. Those entering the grounds were visually assailed with large plywood-painted signs proclaiming "bong the Cong" and "fight-win," serving as a clear reminder that the war in Vietnam should be a decisive fight to victory.

Unsure round-eyed recruits rolled out of buses past a looming entrance to begin two days of orientation and were funneled into a reception area before their eight weeks of basic training began. Heads shaved to the scalp, recruits were poked and prodded by medics, vaccinated, administered aptitude tests, stripped of personal items, and given supplies. At night, nervous young men slept tightly packed in rows of neatly lined World War II–era barracks after being divided into brigades, then platoons. Many young men had not volunteered, being conscripted involuntarily in the draft, unlike my dad. Volunteer or not, no one knew what to expect, and no one was fully prepared for the training that ensued.

Rick Collins was one of the recruits. He would rise at 4:00 a.m. with the other young men and prepare to start his day nervously freezing as they waited in morning formation. The icy cool morning mist transformed to sticky, humid heat as the day progressed. The physical training was intense as recruits were put through their paces with sit-ups, push-ups, jogging, and jumping jacks. They were trained in obedience, weaponry, and equipment, and they endured the seemingly sadistic experience of being locked in a small room with a deployed tear gas grenade. Gasping and groaning, they would emerge from that trial with a small teaspoon-sized taste of the misery of war. Sleep was disrupted, limits were pushed, and recruits were screamed at as every aspect of their endurance was tested, refining and honing it for battle.

Those who survived boot camp and were not recycled back to the beginning graduated from the title of recruit to soldier. Soldiers at Fort Polk underwent advanced infantry training in either Tiger Land or Tiger Ridge.

Five years before my dad, Rick Collins, stepped foot on the Louisiana ground at Fort Polk, the military had given the fort a mission to prepare U.S. Army infantrymen for war in whatever environment they were sent to. This was a mission that they carried out with the full intention of preparing each man for what he would encounter overseas. Tiger Land and Tiger Ridge were formed with years of hard-won knowledge of fighting in Vietnam. The more famous of the two training grounds was marked by a large black painted entrance that bore the words "Tiger Land" in bold orange letters and a large wooden depiction of a tiger ready to pounce menacingly mounted above. Both Tiger Land and Tiger Ridge simulated wartime experiences designed to mimic situations faced by soldiers overseas. Vietnam villages were recreated, complete with thatched huts, animal pens, and underground tunnels. Shallow water features hid tunnels underground, and sharpened punji stakes stood ready to impale. Soldiers with real-life war experience were tasked with pretending to be either friendly citizens or venomous Vietnam Viet Cong enemies. Soldier trainees had to determine friendlies from enemies, navigate booby traps and tripwires, and conduct practice search and destroy missions. The intensity and precision poured into these soldiers were expected to pay off in gains in a war that was fast losing traction.

While my dad was at Fort Polk being marched and molded into a military fighting machine, he received a call that would shake him. His mom had been diagnosed with cancer and needed immediate surgery. He was given a two-week leave to tend to her care and visit with her. While he was away, his squad was sent on orders to Germany. When my dad got back from his leave, his orders read Vietnam.

If he thought Fort Polk was the worst place on earth, my dad was about to enter a far worse hell in the roiling jungles of Vietnam. He boarded an airplane for his first-ever airplane flight. Destination: Fort Lewis, Washington. From there, he made a long flight to Vietnam. He later wrote, "If anyone ever says they weren't afraid in war, they are lying." Rick Collins was a man of courage and a fighter, yet he still recognized the grip of fear. After landing, his first act in Vietnam was the sobering task of filling out his last will and testament to allocate his earthly possessions. Leaving his family behind was foremost in his thoughts. He wanted to make it back to hug his sweetheart Linda and cradle his child in his army-strengthened arms.

My dad was assigned to the 1st of the 27th, Company C of the 25th Infantry Division, the "Wolfhounds." The 1st and 2nd of the 27th are the only groups who can proudly call themselves Wolfhounds. Their motto boasts, "Once a Wolfhound, always a Wolfhound!"

In Vietnam, my dad carried a small Bible signed by his grandma and punctuated with the promise that she would pray for him and the rest of the boys. He recalled, "I carried it with me, and maybe that's why I made it home alive." My dad knew that Jesus was his Savior and that God had a purpose for everything.

Even while sick with cancer, his mom, "Momma," had reinforced this message until it became a piece of him, ingrained in every fabric and fiber of his being. He had grown up in faith, but the war would make him grasp it as never before. His faith would carry him when all else crumbled.

Vietnam was a violent, haunting hellhole of loss and terror, an immense misery of mire and blood far from the lofty ideals stated in the mission of saving the world from the spread of Communism. It was not a fight to win anything; it was a fight to survive. Survival meant personal victory, and this was what mattered to the men draped in mud and blood fighting so as not to see their military brothers killed beside them. Plagued by heat, weighed down by weapons that often failed due to the inhospitable climate, and enduring impossible conditions, each man advanced by sheer strength of will and might of endurance. They had to carry on as if they had not cradled the decimated bodies of their best friends crying in death for their mommas or buried pieces of their brothers in shallow graves marked by grass or crude bamboo crosses. These men are heroes not because they wanted to be but because they had to be.

While the rest of America was safe and sound in their homes preparing for Christmas in 1968, their trees glistening with lights and laughter anointing the air with the holiday spirit, like so many soldiers in Vietnam, my dad longed for a taste of that carefree revelry. The closest thing in Vietnam to Christmas normalcy was the Bob Hope Christmas Show. Soldiers jockeyed for a chance to attend, and my dad was no different from the other men hoping to get an invite. Everyone in the 25th Infantry wanted to go, but my dad was not one of the lucky ones chosen. Instead of being shuttled into the show, he spent Christmas in a foxhole. Assigned in a group of 200 men to an outpost, they would maintain vigil in the hills.

As the day drifted into night, the uneasy silence was interrupted by the sounds of the gathering enemy. Confident that thousands were circling them, my dad clutched his weapon and waited, prepared to go out in a blazing last stand. Thoughts of the Texas Alamo flashed in his head as my dad and the rest of the soldiers prepared to be vastly outmanned and outgunned. A proud Texan, he was committed to fighting until the eternal breath left his body. The sounds of the distant shooting were answered with Wolfhound volleys of fire and light rounds of artillery as an invisible army seemed to be closing in. It was impossible to see them coming as the ink-black sky provided a drape of dark invisibility; they could hear the enemy, and the sounds of their growing force made even the bravest soldiers tremble. They were certain that death awaited all of them.

A shocking discovery was made as the dawn broke, and the infantry emerged from their foxholes to recon and ascertain when the enemy would close in for impending slaughter. Two Viet Cong soldiers were found dead alongside loudspeaker equipment and records of crowd noises. My dad would remember that Christmas in Vietnam as his worst and loneliest, standing vigil against an army formed and fed by fear.

CHAPTER 5

Purposeful Intent

Rivulets of red poured down his face—
a crimson baptism in blood from the wound
that earned him his first Purple Heart.

Most of my dad's wartime memories stayed locked away deep inside. How could he even begin to explain the brutality of bloodshed, the desperate dash to kill or be killed, or the sacred bond with his military brothers—men with whom he had shared meals or traded dark humor-infused jokes in the state of cognizant dissonance needed to survive? These were stories that my dad didn't tell.

However, when pressed, he issued a written account for his children to keep. It was an unemotional narrative of his wartime experience where, just as in life, he humbly downplayed his contributions, highlighting others who served alongside him instead. He noted a medic who dragged him to safety, a general who delivered daily orange soda to him in the hospital, and guards standing on alert watching over the wounded housed in a makeshift tin hospital. These men doing their duty were the heroes he hailed. He admired those who lived with purposeful intent. Ordinary acts done with consistency—these were heroic to him. He lived his life one positive daily decision at a time, so it is no surprise that these were the lessons that left an impression on him.

Purposeful intention was the only way a soldier survived in Vietnam. Each soldier had to find an internal drive to continue forward, putting one foot in front of the other to make gains instead of focusing on the unbearable conditions around him. While barracks housed some soldiers on large fire support bases, army infantrymen like my dad often were entrenched in foxholes covered by tarps or ponchos to protect from the elements. Monsoon rains turned foxholes into watery mud pits that mired the men with trench foot, dysentery, malaria, and other afflictions as the brutal terrain took on its own tactic of attacks. Heat, humidity, and months of rain kept the men drenched, their wet clothes encouraging a bacterial feast on the flesh of their own bodies. Ambushes and hidden mines kept the men on edge, not knowing if their next step would be their last. Natural predators such as poisonous snakes attacked at random, and strained mental deterioration from the enemies who were often not seen assailed the morale of the young men.

The Viet Cong was short on resources but not on ingenuity. An unseen army of farmers, townspeople, and soldiers would rig mines, plant explosives, and set traps before disappearing, leaving only the treads of their tire track sandals as evidence of their appearance. Enemies by night disguised as seemingly friendly civilians by day, the locals were known to attack viciously before blending back in with the rest of the population. Chasing an army of ghosts was unnerving, but the inability to accurately identify the enemy and directly retaliate stripped the men fighting of strength and stability.

One February day, my dad battled an uneasy feeling that was different from the uncertain anxiety that regularly gripped him under the strain of endless missions and heart-wrenching homesickness. He knew deep in his gut that something bad was going to occur. The haunting sickness of fear rested on his shoulders. He pressed onward, trying to put it out of his mind and focus on his men and their mission, but he had felt this feeling before. A few weeks prior, a shell had exploded nearby, raining shrapnel through his helmet. Instinctively, he reached up to rip the burning shrapnel from his skull, the white-hot heat searing his fingers. Rivulets of red poured down his face—a crimson baptism in blood from the wound that earned him his first Purple Heart.

Stitches and a brief hospital stay didn't supersede service, and my father was soon back in the jungle and stricken with that feeling of inevitable impending disaster. Senses on hyper-alert, he was concluding his 130th mission forty miles north of Tay Nen near the Cambodian border. Two platoons of Company C were on patrol, and the *thrum thrum thrum* of a helicopter's blades beat out a comforting pulse as Colonel Reed oversaw their direction from the sky.

Rick Collins was leading a squad of twelve men when they approached a small clearing about thirty yards long. Ordered to direct his squad across the clearing, they started to move out of a thick jungle into the open field. The point man's paces reached the edge of the treeline ahead when they were stunned by an *ambush!* Training took over, adrenaline kicking in to manage the panic as machine-gun fire tore around them and explosions rippled the ground before erupting in a sea of burning flesh, fire, and fear.

A wire appeared at my dad's feet. He tried to turn and yell, "mine!" but the impact of the charge consumed his voice. His legs crumbled beneath him. His hand remained on the trigger of his weapon—a barrage of bullets sprayed from his gun as if protesting the cruelty of the explosion tearing through him. On his knees, he kept firing toward the hidden enemy as his men continued to be felled all around him. The pain of red hot hell ripped at his body as the mine shattered and shredded his legs. Two enemy bullets met their mark in his shoulder, knocking him down before he collapsed into a silent numbness. He could hear nothing but felt the reverberating bullets zing past his head, and he knew that his men were dying in that clearing.

Medic! Medic! Medic! Was his voice calling out for help, or did he imagine the screams? The smells of burning nylon and smoke and the metallic scent of death seared his nostrils as if sickening smelling salts were waking him into war and calling him to consciousness. His body started shaking in shock as a medic crawled to him, firmly gripping his sweat and blood-soaked collar to drag him back to safety. Slowly the medic dragged him pull after bloody pull toward rescue. My dad later wrote, "I wish I could thank that medic, whoever he was." I owe my dad's life to those intentional movements of the heroic medic who did his duty without fail or faltering, and upon delivering my dad to safety, returned valiantly to the fray.

The ongoing firefight kept incoming MEDEVAC helos circling at a distance as other units were called in. The fighting was fierce, and panic masked the faces of those around my dad in the sightless stare of approaching death. Blood shot from my dad's shoulder in scarlet streams. He couldn't see his legs and was uncertain if they were even there. His hearing loss brought a reprieve from the hellish screams and guttural cries sobbing from dying soldiers' throats, but it returned in time for him to hear the men loading him onto transport yell, "If we don't get him out of here, he will die." He knew their words were true.

Medics pumped morphine shots into his chest as he was eagle flighted to a field hospital for rapid stabilization. As the morphine took effect, the world tilted into the barren blackness of nothingness.

Three days later, he woke up in a cast from the chest down. He was alive, but barely.

That horrific day, my dad bravely persisted in his duty, holding nothing back from what he was called to do. The men that fought beside him matched his fortitude, marching forward in their training, even at the highest cost. On February 1, 1969, out of the twelve men in my dad's squad, eight were killed and two were gravely wounded. My dad remarked in his written account, "It was a very bad day."

CHAPTER 6

A Battle to Survive

***Our fingers traced the letters memorializing
the lost as we whispered silent prayers of thanks
that the name of Richard Frank Collins
was not etched on that wall.***

On November 11, 1986, the Vietnam Veteran's Memorial in Washington, DC, was dedicated to all the brave soldiers who gave their lives in combat or were declared missing in action (MIA) in a war that so many struggled to reconcile. A gleaming jet-black granite monument erected in a poignant V-shape is one of the most moving monuments in our nation's capital and was created both to honor and to heal a country scarred by bloodshed on foreign soil. Bearing the names of 58,318 lost men and women, the monument stands as a stark reminder of the eternal sacrifices that so many families made.

Visitors walk through the monument, the heavy weight of sadness, honor, and respect palpable in the faces whose reflections are mirrored back at them in the shiny ebony glow of the granite walls. Every name carved, etched, and memorialized belongs to someone dear. Each one represents a somber soldier's knock on a household door, notifying loved ones that they would never hold or hug their family member again. The cold granite walls remember, but they don't ease the pain of parents who collapsed in agonizing animalistic cries of loss as they were told their son or daughter was never coming home. These walls honor yet do not fill survivors' guilt, fight haunting ghosts of war, or stand in comfort beside those who have lost their closest friends. The Vietnam Veteran's Memorial stoically stands to remind us that freedom is paid in death and sacrifice and that it is our duty never to forget to revere with the highest value that immeasurable cost.

On a crisp spring day in Washington, DC, I had the distinct honor of visiting this stirring monument with my father. Surrounded by my family, my dad rolled in his wheelchair toward the lustrous black granite, where the right wall of the memorial rose with the names of those first lost in Vietnam. His eyes searched the names of friends as tears welled in the gazes of onlookers. Our fingers traced the letters memorializing the lost as we whispered silent prayers of thanks that the my dad's name of Richard Frank Collins was not etched on that wall.

Three days after my dad was eagle flighted from the bloody battlefield ambush to a field hospital for triage, he woke up in a body cast that enshrined him from the chest downward. After stabilization, he was moved to a field hospital in Cu Chi, where he would spend twenty-seven grueling days fighting to stay alive. Both his legs had been completely shattered by the blast of the trip-wired mine. In Cu Chi, the doctors attempted traction to help repair his damaged legs. Still, gangrene set in—the decomposition and putrefaction of the infection, causing doctors to make the difficult decision to amputate. Surgeons would remove his left leg above the knee in an effort to save his life from the spread of infection.

Cu Chi was more field than hospital—tin buildings with rounded metal roofs and an adjacent helicopter pad made up most of the small medical compound. One night, the hospital fell under attack, shrapnel screaming through the walls as the sound reverberated, ripping through the tin and groaning as if entire structures would collapse on the waiting wounded. Patients were hastily covered with flight jackets for protection, and any soldier who could hold a gun was given a rifle. Some of the wounded were quickly hidden under hospital beds. Unable to move from his bed, my dad gripped his assigned gun, ready to fight from his spot. Still trapped in traction with metal rods spearing his remaining leg, my dad had no choice but to face the fight. He could see the hospital guards standing sentinel at the doors with their M-16 machine guns at the ready to try to hold the enemy out, but he couldn't move from his spot to help or escape the attack surrounding him.

Unable to run toward the fight, he had to wait and trust that the soldiers defending the hospital would keep him safe. After all his close encounters with wartime death, this memory remained seared in his mind as the most terrifying. He later wrote about that night, "This night was the scariest of my life . . . fortunately, we fought the Viet Cong off." Although saved from that attack, my dad was still fighting. He was battling to survive and to keep from succumbing to his wounds.

A series of surgeries were buoyed by an onslaught of needed blood transfusions that infected my dad with a severe bout of malaria. Critically hurt and critically ill, my dad deliriously wished for death as malaria racked his body with chills, muscle aches, and painful high fevers. His fever was dangerously high and showed no signs of breaking. His only chance of survival was an urgent flight to Japan.

Once in Japan, doctors resorted to wheeling his wounded body outside on a stretcher and packing his body with snow and ice to try to save his life. Military planes flew in and out of the skies above him as he wished his soul would be set free from the confines of his wrecked body to soar into heavenly rest. Death swooped and soared around him like the planes overhead, but it didn't take my dad. After two hours in the snow, his fever lifted, and he was carried inside, weak yet alive.

My dad's wound from the amputation was left open in an attempt to clear the infection. Changing the gauze and sterile dressings became a regular excruciating process, threatening his ability to endure. In his writing about that period, there is only one moment of brightness in the dark skies of that season of recovery. As he explained, "The head of the medical doctors, a general (I wish I could remember his name), would visit me every day and bring me orange sodas. They tasted so good, but I wasn't able to eat; I was so weak."

He spent weeks there, his body wasting away. Every day was a gamble to see if he would make it to the next morning. Typically a robust 180 pounds, my dad was a frail shadow of himself, losing over half his body weight as he shrank to a skeletal ninety pounds. In Japan, his wound was closed, and he was finally flown back to the United States for further care.

Rick would wisely recall, "Through this early recovery process, I realized that my life would never be the same again, but also realized that there were so many other guys worse off than I was, and I shouldn't feel sorry for myself. God had protected me over there and allowed me to get home."

CHAPTER 7

When the Fighting Gets Tough, the Tough Fight Harder

Resilience sparked determination and toughness to see the odds as irrelevant to him.

Rick hadn't spoken to his family since before the ambush. A stream of telegrams had kept them apprised of his condition, but they longed to hear his voice and receive the reassurance that would bring. A transfer from the hospital in Japan brought him to a brief two-day stay at a military base in California. There he would finally be able to call home himself.

Situated in a private room on the army base, he was treated like a king. Served steak with all the trimmings followed by cake and ice cream, he couldn't muster the strength to chew, so he focused his energy on savoring the small servings of creamy delight. He was so weak that lifting even the lightest item was a strain, but that didn't stop him from picking up the phone to dial home. In the days of high long-distance phone charges, my dad was allocated a heavenly fifteen free minutes of daily cherished phone time. He called his wife, Linda. The sound of her voice and that of his family was a healing balm to his soul. It gave him hope and the will to recover.

Soon my dad relayed the news to his family that they all had been hoping for. He was being transferred back to Texas for further care. He arrived at the air base in San Antonio before being placed on a hospital bus to Fort Sam Houston. "Fort Sam," as it was locally nicknamed, had been designated a principal medical training center for the army after World War II. Known as the "Home of Army Medicine" or "Home of the Combat Medic," Fort Sam was a mere six-hour drive from his family in Dallas. This meant my dad would have a steady stream of visitors throughout his stay.

Two of his closest childhood buddies, Rocky Johnson and Ronnie Cochran, were stationed at the air base, serving as medics. When they found out that my dad was scheduled to arrive at their base, they lobbied to be allowed to meet him. Overcome with excitement, they unloaded him from the transport, forgetting to lock the legs of the stretcher. It collapsed, spilling him onto the ground, body cast and all. They were horrified as waves of fresh pain rippled through his broken body. My dad teasingly reminded them of this incident for decades to come. Although he was in intense pain worsened by their accidental folly, my dad was so grateful to see the familiar faces of his buddies welcoming him back home.

Rick was soon enveloped in the loving greetings and concerned welcomes of his wife Linda, his son Ricky Lynn, his mom and dad, Uncle Marvin, Aunt Betty, Uncle Gene, Aunt Valeria, and others who had all turned out to meet him. The support of his family and their visits made the next several months of hospitalization bearable. My dad was back in Texas but was still a long way from recovery.

Still weak from weight loss and diminishing muscle mass, my dad was placed in the skilled hands of orthopedic surgeon Dr. Hugh Ratliff. Ratliff was a fellow Wolfhound from the Vietnam fields, and his presence brought Rick encouragement. Recognizing Rick from Vietnam, he would continuously remind him, "Wolfhounds are tough." It was a gruff but needed reminder that when the fighting gets tough, the tough fight harder. That is precisely what my dad did.

Though physically weakened, my dad would have to rally all the inner strength he had to face his next round of surgeries. The doctors gave him a grim choice: they could amputate his remaining right leg since the knee was gone and irreparably shattered, or they could fuse it stiff where the knee joint had been. If fused, he was cautioned that he would be confined to a wheelchair and would never be able to walk again. My dad wrote, "I thought a fused leg was better than no leg at all, so that's what we did."

The surgery took place while my dad was fully awake. Dosed only with pain shots, he was placed on a table that tilted to force or fuse the bones in the leg and knee together. He screamed in agonizing distress as the bones shuddered and crunched together. The sounds of the wrenching bones cracked loudly enough for him to hear. Once again, Dr. Ratliff stoically reminded him, "Wolfhounds are tough." My dad could only move forward, which is what he was determined to do.

Rick would later recall, despite this torturous procedure, "What has always stayed with me from the moment I was in San Antonio at the hospital was how fortunate I found myself." Surrounded by boys who had lost multiple limbs and around-the-clock cries of severely burned soldiers screaming in tortured pain, my dad knew that despite his difficult circumstances, he was still surrounded by blessings. He clung to gratefulness even while acknowledging his helplessness to comfort those in agony around him. He wrote:

> Their cries at night would keep me up, and all I could do was pray to God to have mercy on them. I would think about my wife, Linda, and our son Ricky Lynn and how I couldn't wait to be back at home with them and all my family. I felt lucky somehow. I saw many guys' wives come in and serve them divorce papers because they just couldn't deal with what their futures would be like with disabled amputees or severely burned husbands. It broke my heart, and I knew that I was lucky. I also knew that my life would be a struggle, but I would

beat the odds and was going to walk and not be confined to a wheelchair.

My dad displayed a remarkable ability to seek out gratefulness in any situation or circumstance. When others wouldn't have been able to see past their pain, my dad counted his blessings. This gratefulness, when nurtured by the support of his family and friends, allowed him to draw from a deep well of resilience. Resilience sparked determination and toughness to see the odds as irrelevant to him. After all, his identity was not shaped by his circumstances; it was shaped by him. Wolfhounds were tough, but I dare say that Rick Collins was the toughest. He was built to beat the odds, but it wouldn't be easy. He knew that it would be a momentous challenge, yet no one could have predicted the heart-wrenching pain and loss that was about to occur.

CHAPTER 8

Bravely Battling

Discussing the things we would rather hide takes a lot of strength.

Rick spent six months recovering at Fort Sam Houston, from the summer of June 1969 until December of that same year. He was then moved to a Veteran's Affairs (VA) hospital in Dallas. Finally back in his hometown, he focused his energy on the task doctors had told him would be impossible—learning to walk.

His left leg was amputated, and his remaining right leg was now fused straight in a manner that reminded him of a peg leg. His right foot remained, but it hung limp and useless, unable to function like a typical foot. He spent hours upon hours working to rehabilitate it, a belt tied around it to pull it back and forth to try to tame it into usefulness. His appetite gradually returned as he began to rebuild strength and a more robust physical structure. After months of work, he achieved his goal. Finally, after much effort and persistence, he walked! A wobbly, labored jaunt assisted by crutches, my dad was thrilled to do the feat doctors denied he could accomplish. This gave him a stronger sense of self-assurance that he would regain some semblance of his former self. He would move forward, and he could beat the odds. This empowered him!

His increasing mobility was nearly overshadowed by magnified difficulty surrounding him. When

World War II veterans returned home from war, there were ticker-tape parades, celebratory reveling, and free drinks flowing. These U.S. soldiers returning home from World War II were cast as clear victors in an epic showdown between good and unadulterated evil. Rick had grown up worshipping his own war heroes—his favorite uncles who served as larger-than-life representations of the honor these men acclaimed. Rick didn't return home from Vietnam expecting a hero's welcome, but he did imagine his service would afford some level of respect and kindness to the returning soldiers.

Unfortunately, he experienced much the opposite. Many Americans viewed Vietnam through the lens of a political pawn game in which the governmental players wanted to press forward in a blazing show of force against the evils of communism. They expected to strike hard and fast, gaining a definitive score for democracy. This did not occur, and the nation couldn't help but reel as vivid photo images displaying the barbaric nature of war were splashed across news broadcasts and magazines.

The unpopularity of this seemingly unending war was bleeding into the collective fabric of our nation. A stain of blood turned black on the nation's righteous reputation. Protests swelled and rhetoric ramped up as tensions boiled. Conscripted soldiers who fought without choice were now taunted and mocked as many misplaced their blame upon them. My dad had volunteered to fight but had not chosen the battlefield. His service was in respect to the decisions of those elected, and he expected that, at a minimum, others would understand and acknowledge this.

Modern historians try to downplay or minimize the painful receptions that Vietnam veterans experienced upon returning home, characterizing them as outlying occurrences that became branded in the nation's mind as truth. However, my dad's experiences and those of countless others prove that gaslighting our country's pain would not serve to heal a nation saturated with the heavy tears of trauma that tolled on the generation living under the dark shadow of the Vietnam War.

Rick would document his own difficult experiences by writing:

Sadly, during these next months, times when I was in public or before I could walk and I was in a VA Hospital wheelchair, people would spit and yell at me. One day I went with a buddy to a downtown Dallas café where a young guy started screaming at me, "Murderer, you murderer! Killers, all of you are killers!" My buddy slugged the guy, and we were asked to leave. This was painful and something that really hurt me. When I got back, I saw all the stories about how the United States soldiers were dopeheads, murderers, and rapists. There may have been isolated incidents, and people think everyone was like that. I was there; I fought. Nobody I saw or was with was a dopehead. I didn't see murdering or raping going on. It really made me upset, really upset when I heard people say those things. I look back on that time and just didn't want to talk about the war or that my injuries were even related to fighting. I was proud of my service and those that fought with me. I felt I was fighting for freedom and democracy over there.

My dad succinctly expressed what so many soldiers were feeling. They had served their country faithfully and yet were scorned as the bad guys. They were suffering from trauma, as many soldiers do, but that didn't mean they were suddenly unfeeling monsters. Yet, many brave soldiers returned home cloaked in an inescapable mantle of shame deposited on them by the anger of others.

My dad's initial postwar interactions with civilians caused him to shy away from discussing his service. He allowed people to incorrectly assume that he had lost his leg due to a bout with childhood polio. This was a relatively common cause of limb disfigurement in his generation. It wasn't until I was school age that I heard my dad recount the actual story of his service, which resulted in the damage to his body.

I am thankful that my dad shrugged off shame and chose to recognize the pride in his service. Pieces of him remained in Vietnam, but he wholly resolved to heal and move forward. I found my dad's service and two Purple Hearts inspirational and often replayed that moment over and over in my mind of hearing him tell his story. I will forever be grateful that my dad could open up about his experiences in the war to my family and me. So many young men and women who have seen the hells of war up close cannot bring themselves to think about it or deal with the tormenting or haunting feelings they carry. Discussing the things we would rather hide takes a lot of strength. When unexamined, these shards of pain pierce our lives, shredding who we are meant to be. My dad was brave enough to share and write about his experiences, and his stories positively impacted all those who heard them.

My dad often credits his family for helping him heal, and when he was finally fully able to go home after seemingly endless hospital stays, he was grateful. He imagined that the hardships earned in Vietnam were in the past and that he could build a better future for his family, despite his physical challenges. With the help of his wife and family, he was making strides toward rebuilding his life.

However, the unthinkable happened on a rainy day in May of 1970. Driving through Dallas with a friend, my dad stared out the passenger window at the dreary day around him. A traffic light reflected in the puddling water around their car as they watched in horror as a braking bus slipped and slid through a red light toward their vehicle. Brakes shrieked, passengers screamed, and metal twisted and moaned in angry protest as the runaway bus ran directly over the car my father was a passenger in. Nearly crushed, Rick's fused leg snapped in half as the vehicle's dashboard caved in on them. The car's steel frame buckled, metal bending in on itself like folds of an accordion. Rick's leg fused straight, crumbled, and shattered in a sickening cacophony of crushing bones and anguished cries.

The accident didn't cost him his right leg, but what he did lose was progress, and he almost lost hope. He had fought for over a year to recover from his Vietnam War wounds. He had recovered from shoulder shrapnel, regained mobility after a body cast, lost a leg to amputation, battled malaria and weight loss, endured excruciating bone setting and surgical procedures, and learned to walk again. All for what? My dad had paid his dues, and his fight was supposed to be over, yet here he was again. Bruised and beaten down, the depression fought to grasp and pull him under permanently. He wrote, "The pain of the injuries and the thought of recovery again were almost too much to take."

Despite this, he pressed onward. Once again, he found himself restrained in a body cast. He would spend six months in this cast at the Dallas VA Medical Center. As his bones slowly repaired, his medical team transitioned him into a leg cast accompanied by the use of a wheelchair. He spent three months recuperating. Amazingly, my dad, Corporal Collins, would later reflect on his war injuries and the subsequent vehicle accident with positivity and strength, "It was a long process from February 1, 1969, until then, but I tried never to be bitter or have self-pity. At this point, I still considered myself a lucky person and have often said that my time in the Army is probably the best thing that ever happened to me."

CHAPTER 9

Angels among Us

*It was as if I had been visited by an angel
in the form of my best friend,
my hero—my dad.*

My dad walked toward me on two healthy legs, his green eyes sparkling with radiant joy that was echoed in his gleaming smile. He looked young, vibrant, and strong. He appeared as if he were in his thirties, handsome and whole, bounding with an energy and excitement that I had never witnessed before. He had certainly never been physically whole in my lifetime. All I had known was his broken body, a series of surgeries, and his daily battle with physical pain. I had never seen him like this before. He spoke with me, assuring me that he was good—he was whole. I woke knowing that he was with me, amazed at the clarity of my dream and the wave of supernatural peace it brought me. It was as if I had been visited by an angel in the form of my best friend, my hero—my dad.

In December 2020, my dad passed away after a long, full life. The loss of his rich presence and friendship left me languishing in a dark chasm of sadness. His vivid appearance in that dream lifted me out of the gloom and into a state of calm acceptance.

I was not the only one he visited in a dream. Within a day of his appearance to me, my sister Caryn had a similar experience in which he came to her in complete clarity in a dream to assure her that he was safe and whole.

The amazing thing was that our experience wasn't unique to us; my dad had experienced a similar supernatural occurrence decades before in a period of excruciating loss.

By November of 1970, my dad had rehabilitated from his car accident to return home and rebuild a life for himself and his family. He had spent much time separated from them due to the war and his injuries, and he was ready to remedy that by building a better life for them. Declared 100 percent disabled, he was able to retire from the U.S. Army and put his VA benefits and pension to work. Settling in Garland, Texas, just northeast of Dallas, his uncles helped him build a house for his young family in close proximity to his larger network of support.

By February 1971, my dad's leg cast was removed, and he focused on rebuilding his strength. He had a pool added to his backyard so he could swim, regaining musculature and creating a strong upper body that would sustain him as he walked, assisted by crutches. He valued independence and felt that a wheelchair limited and restrained him, so he made it his mission to be strong enough to stay out of one. He managed to live up to this personal challenge for fifty years, navigating expertly on his trusted crutches.

Just as he was adjusting to his new normal, resolving to live in this new season of life with strength and fortitude, tragedy struck. His lovely wife, the beautiful twenty-two-year-old Linda Faye, their three-year-old son Ricky Lynn, and his mother-in-law Evelyn Joyce Mayhall were killed in a horrific car accident.

On the morning of November 7, 1971, Linda, Ricky Lynn, and Evelyn waved goodbye to my dad before heading out on what was planned to be a fun visit to some of Linda's extended family in Mississippi. Around 7:00 p.m. that evening, my dad would receive a call that would absolutely crush him. The vehicle that held his mother-in-law, Rick's beautiful high school sweetheart, and their son had been hit in a head-on collision about five hours outside of Dallas. They had been driving on U.S. Highway 80 in Tendal, Louisiana, when a drunk driver crossed into their lane. The driver's large truck decimated their smaller vehicle, killing all of them instantly.

In that one horrible call, my dad's life came crashing down around him. Grief tore through him like a hurricane ripping through anything left of his battered body and spirit. *Why? Why this? Why them?* Rick had already fought through so much pain, yet this pain was incomparable. His scars, surgeries, and deformities—these were all personal pains that he could manage, but the pain of losing everyone that he loved was too much.

Why God, why? He cried out in agony again and again. *Haven't I already been through enough? What had I done to receive this torment? If I deserved to be punished, my precious family did not. Surely an innocent child shouldn't be ripped from his father!* My dad seethed and screamed, protested and yelled, cried and begged, and let loose a torrent of unending questions and accusations to a God who suddenly seemed so far away. Any hope that Rick had held onto was gone, replaced with hollow darkness permeating every part of his being.

Rick's cousin Ronnie accepted the agonizing task of driving to Louisiana to prepare everything for the return of the bodies and their final resting places following a funeral in Dallas. Though present, my dad was like a shadow. He was there but not there, seen but not seen, a spiritless shell in a world that had gone dark around him.

Like a modern-day Job, Rick had been stripped of everything he valued. He had given his body to the war, but that was a willing sacrifice. His heart had been torn from him as he laid his cherished ones to rest. His resilient spirit was replaced with an unimaginable, gnawing, building pain that paralyzed him, ripping the very will to breathe from his broken body. He couldn't fathom where God was in this or why He would allow this to happen.

Researchers often refer to extreme grief as complicated grief—an acute form of debilitating grief persisting at least six months after a death. The intensity of this grief exposes itself in the symptom of yearning for the loved one(s) so penetrating that it keeps a person from participating in other life moments or interests. A once vibrant and colorful life is shaded in greyscale, a painful cycle in which life has no meaning and is bereft of any joy. Complicated grief is often accompanied by drinking, drug abuse, and suicide. I am sure that my dad contemplated each of these ideas of escape daily as he existed in an endless haze of hurt and sorrow.

I am certain that intrusive thoughts about death were constantly on my dad's mind. He had seen friends in Vietnam blown to pieces, had comforted others as they died in his arms, and now felt utterly destroyed by the loss of his sweet wife and son. He was consumed with sadness and survivor's guilt, wondering why he was still alive if this was the outcome.

Rick's mom, Ruth, or "Momma" to him, was so concerned about his state of emotional turmoil and distress that she moved in with him to try to help him cope with his grief. Momma would minister to him and try to keep his daily needs cared for so that his sadness and depression didn't pull him under inescapable darkness. She prayed for him and read her Bible as she stood in as sentry on what she feared was a daily suicide watch. She could feel his pain but trusted that just as in the book of Job, God would intervene with promise. Like a ministering angel, Momma tended to him with comfort and confident support, nurturing him physically and emotionally in the valley of his grief.

Nightly, my dad would weep himself into an exhausted turbulent sleep. His dreams were haunted by the loss of loved ones and tormented by ghoulish visages from Vietnam; he cried out for comfort, asking God to intervene.

During the most intense night of his grief, my dad's life changed forever. As he slept, he was awoken by a soft female voice. His eyes adjusted to the room's darkness just enough to see his wife standing in the corner. Though passed away, she was present with him that night. She spoke to him gently, her sweet voice full of comfort: "Ricky Lynn and I are with God." She assured my dad that she and Ricky Lynn were safe in the arms of their heavenly Father. They were together with God. She told my dad that he would be okay. She gave him reassurance and comfort.

When he awoke, he cried out for Momma, and she came running to his room. She found him sobbing, repeating that God had his loves and wanted him to know everything would be okay. Momma immediately began praising God because she knew that the Lord had met him in that room and that his heart would be able to heal and rest in the knowledge and comfort that his family was safe in heaven. That night, my dad was filled with indescribable supernatural peace, and the next day he awoke with the hope in his heart that he could live his life fully again.

Momma rejoiced for my dad because she knew that the Lord was doing a new work in him, but even as she praised, she began to pray that God would bring another angel into his life. Momma was "Nanny" to me, and Nanny told me that she prayed every day that God would bring someone into my dad's life who would see him beyond his physical and emotional scars and love him fully. Her prayers were answered sooner than she ever expected.

CHAPTER 10

Healing Hope

**Refined through hardship,
his heart wasn't redefined by hurt.**

"Your mom is an angel sent from God to your dad," Nanny would repeat every time I saw her, which was frequently since we lived less than twenty miles from her when I was growing up.

As hope returned to my dad, his world became brighter. The darkness lifted, and rays of sunny light filtered through. Once again, he pulled himself up, onward, and forward. Again, his experiences echoed those of biblical Job, but this time instead of a season of loss, my dad entered into the hope of restoration.

His friends and family noticed the change and worked to help him experience new moments of joy and delight. In this spirit, Rick's cousin Ronnie Fitzgerald invited my dad out to a company dinner. Several of Ronnie's co-workers from LTV, a defense company based in Dallas-Fort Worth, were gathering for a night out. Boisterous young men and women joined the dinner and were seated randomly around the table.

My dad was placed directly across from a stunningly attractive young woman named Linda Jean Meadows. Linda was beautiful and intelligent, and she maintained the sweetest demeanor. My dad was instantly smitten.

It seemed that Linda Meadows was the angel that Nanny had been praying for. At that first dinner, she saw my dad—truly saw him. Linda saw beyond his physical and emotional scars to the man he was created to be. Where others saw wounds and brokenness, she saw his character and heart. His scars were just scars to her, but they weren't him. They were undoubtedly pieces of him, things that shaped him, but they didn't define him. She recognized the real him.

The tenacity, resilience, and fighting Fitzgerald spirit made him far more than the shell of his body. Refined through hardship, his heart wasn't redefined by hurt. It was made stronger by the strength of his scars. She recognized that instantly. He recognized it, too, because something about her just made them click. It was as if God smiled down and gifted Rick the angel that my nanny had been praying for.

Operating hand controls to maneuver his vehicle, Rick drove Linda home that first night. Capable and confident, he navigated the dark roads with her by his side. This was something that they would do for years to come—driving and dreaming together for their future. Only six days apart in age, they both sensed that they had been placed together for something unique, and from that moment on, they were inseparable. Filled with deep gratitude for each other, they both knew that the grace of God had brought them together.

When they celebrated their twenty-fifth anniversary in 1997, my mom wrote this poem that captured their relationship perfectly:

My Gift

It seems like only yesterday
When all my dreams came true,
When God smiled down upon my life
And gave me the gift of you.

Maybe He saw you had a need,
And knew I had one too—
But from the moment that we met—
We knew!

You are my strength, my guide in life,
You show me the way when I am low.
You taught me what is important in life
From that path you'd have to go.

Your strength is my shadow and always will be,
Your smile is in spite of your pain,
Your love of life and family is beyond compare,
And you don't see loss; you see gain.

The time we share grows more precious each day,
And our life together is blessed in so many ways!
If only everyone could have a life's love so true...
That's why I thank God for the gift of you.

I will always love you!

My dad told me many times that he was the luckiest man ever to live because God gave him two "loves of his life." Ironically, both were named Linda. Both Lindas were beautiful, had a vivacious zest for life, and loved my dad. He had lost his first precious Linda but knew that God had extraordinarily gifted him by bringing him another chance at a loving future. My dad needed my mom, and she needed him. Within a few weeks of dating, they both knew that this love would be forever. Nanny's prayers were answered, and my mom would remain by my dad's side for the next forty-eight years.

Before my parents got married, my mom called her parents in Jal, New Mexico. She wanted them to meet the man that she had grown to love so much. She couldn't imagine a future without them but wanted her parents' approval to start things off right.

My grandfather, OE Meadows, was a very astute judge of character and intention. A prominent community leader and local businessman, he was wise to the good and evils of the world. As he listened to my mom describe the man she wanted them to meet as she saw a future with him, he and my grandmother became immediately concerned.

My grandparents both worried that my mom's compassionate heart and caring personality made her susceptible to a situation that would entrap her. They feared she felt sorry for Rick and misread these empathetic feelings as an emotional connection. They assumed that he was carrying a lot of physical and emotional baggage, and they did not want the weight of that placed on their cherished daughter. After expressing their concerns, she quipped, "He won't let me feel sorry for him, and he won't let anyone else, including you." She knew my dad did not have a personality that allowed him to be pitied. He carried himself with strength and fortitude that she knew her parents would recognize.

"I am bringing him home to meet you," she confidently declared. Rick and Linda traveled to the small city of Jal, New Mexico, on the western Texas border, and met her parents. My parents were married on August 21, 1972, within two whirlwind months of meeting each other.

They quickly settled into the rhythm of married life and began planning to grow their family together. My dad had been given many limits by doctors. They didn't think he would survive his war wounds, but he did. They had told him that he would never regain the ability to walk, but he did. So, when they told him that he wouldn't be able to have children due to the trauma of his injuries, he figured that that wouldn't stop him from building a family. My parents decided to start the process of adoption. He and my mom filled out copious amounts of paperwork applying to adopt a child.

Their application to adopt submitted, they were stunned to learn that my mom was pregnant. My mom was expecting a baby. She was pregnant with me! Somehow my dad had defied the odds once again.

As a small child, I often wondered what it was like for my dad to learn the news that he would be a father again. He had lost a wife and a son, but he had also gained a wife and a son. This must have brought an array of mixed emotions. I would ask him about it, and he would tell me that he genuinely believed God knew him personally, which meant that the Lord knew exactly what my dad needed. God didn't just see my dad, but He knew the desires of his heart, and he richly fulfilled them. He had brought my dad from the precipice of what felt like hell to a fulfilling, renewed lease on life.

My birth in 1973 brought great joy to both my parents, and it was followed up four years later, in

1977, with the birth of my sister Caryn Ann. My dad was over the moon! He was thrilled to have defied the birth odds once, but twice was an even greater blessing. He loved us both fiercely and with an appreciation born of much loss. He didn't take the gift of our lives for granted. My sister and I were equally blessed to be raised by two of the most incredible parents anyone could ever ask for.

Nanny always called my mom an angel sent to my dad, but the truth is that we are all blessed with angels in our lives if we let them in and recognize them. In a spiritual sense, God definitely brought peace to my father, Caryn, and me through the gift of seemingly angelic dreams after the passing of our loved ones. In a practical sense, God sent caring and compassionate humans to minister to my dad and help him through life. These were his angels. Momma (Nanny to me) was one of them. She prayed for him faithfully and tended to his care when he needed compassion the most. She was a constant source of steady encouragement for him throughout his lifetime. As Nanny always said, my mom was another angel in my dad's life. She walked beside him and pushed him to live a full, rich life, complete with laughter and love. She didn't feel sorry for him; she knew he was someone to be envied for his strength, persistence, and character. They made a fantastic team and left a legacy of impact that will forever be felt by future generations of Collins children and relatives.

My dad was blessed to be surrounded by these sweet angels, but he also had the wisdom to open his heart and life to new love and experiences. He had every right to be bitter and angry and to feel entitled, but he chose to see life with grace and opportunity. If the darkness of his difficulty had caused him to close off his life to the possibility of love and light, he would have missed out on all the beauty that God had in store for Him. God endlessly redeemed and restored his life, writing new chapters that left an impact on all those privileged to know Rick Collins.

CHAPTER 11

Never Quit

My dad was wise enough not to reside in the past yet still learn from it.

My dad was experiencing abundant good in his life, but that did not mean that he was without challenge. Every day was a battle against an onslaught of constant, chronic pain. Each moment he was torn between memories of his painful past and his new, bright future.

My dad was wise enough not to reside in the past yet still learn from it. This allowed him to remain grateful, grasp the present, and celebrate its joys. While he reveled in the life of a newlywed with a burgeoning family, he wanted to accomplish more.

Rick had retired from the Army and received a pension, but he felt a strong need to be useful in a work setting. He didn't want anyone to feel sorry for him, so he obtained his GED and tried to find a job. Injuries aside, losing the ability to have an identifiable purpose or mission in daily life is exceptionally traumatic for most veterans working toward creating a new normal. The need for purpose drove my dad to live life as fully as possible.

My dad didn't want to accept a pension if he could work in some capacity. He didn't want to lose his pension either, but by rule, if he could work, he couldn't keep his pension. Most people would have been content with maintaining their pension and living out a retirement life, but my dad wasn't most people. He was determined to work, even if it cost him his pension.

He went on job interview after interview, but it always yielded the same response. The interviewers liked him and his energy, and they admired his excitement to work, but they could not provide him health insurance because of all his disabilities. They would tell him that he was too much of a risk to take on.

These rejections seemed discouraging, but they formed a foundation for a future blessing that my dad would not have expected. I don't think potential employers could read the future, but their concerns manifested. My dad had over forty major surgeries throughout his adult life due to his original war injuries. Rejection from those jobs protected him as he could remain covered by his pension and medical insurance with the VA.

Despite not getting the jobs he had interviewed for, my dad was not one to feel sorry for himself. My mom wouldn't allow anyone to feel sorry for him, either. She wisely got involved, issuing a course of action that would change my dad's trajectory forever.

"You said you liked baseball and football, right?" my mom queried. She had just gotten home for the day when she sprung a new plan on my dad.

My dad affirmed with a nod that he had expressed a love for those sports. He keenly missed being active in the athletics of his teenage years.

Without missing a beat, my mom declared, "Well, I just signed you up to coach a youth football team. I also told the Garland Youth Sports association that you will be coaching football in the fall, too."

Stunned, my dad instantly agreed. I am quite sure that my mom didn't give him a choice, but my dad didn't protest, either. That spring in the year of my birth, the legend of Coach Collins began.

He started coaching with the help of a Fitzgerald family member—his cousin, Bobby. They coached baseball together for several years.

For football, he teamed up to coach with one of his old Vietnam buddies, Butch King. He met Butch in Vietnam when Rick dove into a foxhole in the middle of a firefight. There he would come face to face with Butch as they both hunkered down in the protection of their hole as bullets whizzed and thunked around them. Bonded by battle, they were both trying to navigate new starts.

Butch had played football at Texas A&M before his time in the Army, and like my dad, he was eager to reconnect with the game that he loved. They made a great team, and their shared war experiences brought a unique camaraderie to the gridiron.

My dad was an incredible coach and attracted other great men in Allen, Texas, to coach with him, like Roger Chaney, Charlie Chandler, Glen Renfro, and Dave Whitten, to name a few. An astute teacher of the game, he also taught his players life lessons that they carried with them on and off the field. He was an inspiration in how he approached the responsibility of coaching and the energy he brought. Parents bought in, and players loved him.

A teacher and coach in every sense of the word, my dad lived the "never quit" attitude. He led with a quiet strength that others saw and responded instantly to. He didn't lecture or preach; he simply lived an extraordinary life that others respected as authentic and genuine. This gave his words a weight that resonated with those he coached. There was trust in his insight because his knowledge was hard won.

His players knew that the words "don't quit" from Coach Collins were backed by a brave life of acting intentionally and never giving up. It was evident in the strange torque-fueled motion of his uneasy crutch-assisted walk that took great effort for him. He knew his physical limitations better than anyone and the unrelenting exhaustion of existing in constant pain, yet he never stopped. He always took the high road and didn't waste his life feeling sorry for himself. He didn't play a victim role; he lived life victoriously as an overcomer and modeled this for everyone around him.

My dad always took the time to help others on or off the field. He was grateful for his family, friends, and life, and he found ways to implement living his gratitude. My dad would be the first person to jump to the aid of others physically, emotionally, or financially. This inspired others who thought *If Rick can do it, so can we.*

My dad couldn't move as fast as most people, but he moved anyway. He could no longer compete athletically, but he could coach others who could. He couldn't control his circumstances, but he could manage his attitude and approach to the daily grind of life.

Rather than mourn the things he couldn't control, my dad worked to maintain the things he could. He woke up trying to find things to make him feel as normal as possible. Normality is why he found coaching others to be such a strong motivator for him. His ability to shine his positive outlook and uplift others was a direct reflection of his positive attitude. He had an uncanny ability to build confidence in others by lifting their self-esteem. He always believed in people to the point of directly telling someone, whether a youth or adult, "You can do it."

To this day, I hear from former youth players that he coached saying, "Your dad gave me confidence and believed in me." It has stuck with them their entire lives. He had a gift of controlling what he could control and never quitting when things were tough.

CHAPTER 12

Attitude, Effort, and Coachability

A positive attitude brings possibility, which leads to greater success.

After my sister was born, my parents decided to spread their wings and acreage by purchasing a larger home and property near Allen, Texas. Our little family moved to a small homestead with just over three acres, where we would begin raising horses, goats, and chickens.

An idealistic setting for children to grow up in, there was something magical to me about that ranch home. Memories were formed there, but more importantly, so was my love of football. Our front yard at the ranch seemed gigantic when viewed from my childhood perspective. A large front yard, about fifty-by-fifty yards, made an improvised football field. A tree in each corner marked the boundaries as if permanent pylons for my personal stadium. This patch of grass in my front yard is where I first learned to play football.

I understand my dad's passion for football because I lived it. I didn't just love football; I absorbed every part of it deep into my being. The smell of fresh cut grass, the sting of sweat dripping into my eyes—running, hitting, and running again—my body ached to play the game. I loved the drive of competition, the effort, and the pain that paid off in growth. I craved football and felt great joy and fulfillment from being on that field.

My dad's role as Coach Collins wasn't limited to children in the community. His coaching extended to me as well. I learned many valuable lessons on and off the field from him, but three lessons always stand out in my mind. They are: attitude, effort, and being coachable. These are the lessons that I have also worked hard to instill in my children, and gratefully, they have grasped their grandfather's legacy.

Attitude. My dad taught me early on the importance of having a positive attitude. My dad had every reason not to have a positive attitude. He could have viewed life with distrust and every scenario with the possibility of pain or worst-case results. However, as always, my dad operated with intentionality. He would honestly evaluate a situation with a measured dose of realism, but if the scale was tipping between positive and negative perceptions, he always chose the positive. This taught me to see challenges personally and professionally as an opportunity to achieve things others might not be able to or are unwilling to do. A positive attitude brings possibility, which leads to greater success.

I always try to see the best in people and situations. My life reflects that because my dad modeled this so effectively for me. My dad had an infectious laugh and a smile that would brighten any situation. People noticed and admired this. They expected that his injuries would lead to a dour personality, but he radiated joy. He became his grateful attitude personified, and there was something about it that resonated deeply with everyone.

His smile caused others to light up, his positive spirit illuminating them and powerfully impacting others. I learned from this that a simple gesture like a smile could cast joy on others.

My dad's life was full of hardship and setbacks. These shaped his character and taught all of us around him valuable lessons. Gratefully, my life has had very few setbacks or earth-shattering hardships. My dad worked hard to protect me from them, but when I faced difficulties or challenges, I attacked them with a positive attitude.

My dad, Coach Collins, was the king of the positive attitude—he never gave up hope of a comeback, a miraculous play, or an amazing touchdown. When we focus on the positive, there is always a chance of winning.

Rick loved the Dallas Cowboys, as do all Texans, and we'd talk about the Cowboys' 1975 playoff victory over the Minnesota Vikings as an example. The Cowboys were coming off a very disappointing season, not even making the playoffs. They were also losing marquee players Bob Lilly, Bob Hayes, and Calvin Hill, among others. Everyone around probably feared the dynasty was coming to an end. But the team worked overtime and pushed hard through the season until a cold December 28 when, with seconds remaining in the game, Roger Staubach threw a miraculous fifty-yard touchdown pass to Drew Pearson. Afterward, Staubach called the miraculous touchdown a "Hail Mary," thus cementing the term for a desperation pass in the sports lexicon. Often in football, if one team gets behind, the players fall into despair and lose hope that they can ever win. When this occurs, the game is lost due to a permeating attitude of defeat. For many people, setbacks, challenges, trauma, or tragedy can quickly spiral into a negative attitude, making it seem as if the difficulties cannot be overcome. The Cowboys didn't let that happen, and neither did Rick. Rick was the Roger Staubach of my life and the lives of so many others around him.

A positive attitude doesn't mean abandoning the reality of the situation. It simply means finding hope and learning from the challenge so that you have a greater chance of overcoming the obstacles instead of succumbing to them. We must daily choose to view the world through the lens of a positive attitude. This improves our chances of successfully navigating our setbacks and difficult circumstances.

Effort. Emulating my dad has been at the fore-front of my mind in every endeavor I have pursued.

We often associate effort with career performance or business acumen, but my dad didn't have a job like the other dads I grew up around. Even so, my dad taught me more about effort than anyone I knew. He put strong effort and pride into every single thing that he did. He modeled a work ethic, attention to detail, and principles of outworking others. As I have implemented these traits, they have helped me to be incredibly successful in my own endeavors.

My dad's effort each day was both humbling and inspiring. We take so many things for granted that my dad struggled to work through or overcome. I often marveled at the effort it took for my dad to lift himself out of bed each morning. His remaining leg fused into locked stiffness, and maneuvering in and out of bed, chairs, or into a car became a grueling task. There was no easy answer to the process. He had to expend maximum effort for even minimal results.

For many years, my dad wore an extremely heavy plaster artificial leg in place of his missing limb. My dad would first cover the stump of his leg in a heavy wool sock before he began the arduous task of affixing the prosthesis to his body. He had to delicately position himself in the precise position to slide his stump into his artificial leg before using his dresser as a counterweight to lever himself up from the bed and into a standing position. None of us were strong enough to lift him, so he had no choice except to learn how to manage for himself.

Once upright, my dad's struggle to ready himself for the day wasn't over. Without being able to bend his remaining knee, my dad had to reach down to wrangle his pants over the prosthesis or fasten the belts and buckles that held it up. Putting on pants was immensely challenging, but pulling on a shirt was equally complicated. When bullets had shredded my dad's shoulder in Vietnam, healing resulted in a minimal range of motion in that extremity. Donning a shirt became a daily effort-filled wrestling match with a fabric foe.

Once dressed in a shirt, pants, and prosthesis, Rick faced the daunting task of putting his shoes on. For someone that didn't have the use of bending knees, everything was tough about getting shoes on or tying them. The effort was exhausting. Getting out of bed and dressed each day was a process that took my dad at least an hour. While it might take me five minutes to get dressed on a slow day, my dad's experience was just the opposite. Even so, he was adamant that others not help him do basic things.

At the end of each day, my dad had to repeat the arduous dressing process in reverse. He always persisted, even when it was exhausting. It was imperative to my dad that he kept a certain amount of independence and autonomy. To ensure this, Coach Collins put himself through training paces. He lifted weights and swam daily, knowing that the constant torque on his body for even simple tasks was extreme, and for this, he needed to stay strong. He needed the full strength of his upper body to compensate for the compromised state of his lower extremities.

Growing up, I loved going to the gym to watch my dad lift weights. It was incredible. He gained so much joy and confidence from feeling strong. He could bench press over 400 pounds until well after the age of fifty. To bench press effectively, the weight lifter must have balance with both legs on the ground. For my dad, what remained of his legs didn't operate normally, which made his strength even more impressive. I marveled at his accomplishments.

My dad's effort didn't end with caring for himself and his family. Every day, he purposed to pursue his mission of helping others through coaching. He coached teams year-round and volunteered for leadership roles in youth sports leagues and as an elected trustee of a municipality. Despite his physical limitations, he always approached tasks with maximum effort and pride in his work. This taught me never to shy away from investing significant effort in anything I set out to accomplish. Whether it was school, athletics, or professional endeavors, I learned to take pride in investing my complete effort and reaping the fruit of the results.

Being coachable. The characteristic of being coachable was a huge lesson that my dad continually instilled in me and others. He taught my sister and me to be humble yet confident. An air of confidence was complete only if accompanied by an eagerness to learn and accept that there is always more that you don't know than what you do know. My dad nurtured a sense of curiosity in both of his children. He valued education, and he valued learning experientially from others. He taught us to be lifelong learners.

My dad had limited formal education but made up for it with an eager desire to learn and be coachable. He was constantly growing personally and expected his children to do the same. It is impossible to succeed without humility, curiosity, and the ability to accept wisdom and coaching from others.

My dad had great respect for the uncles, coaches, and principals who took the time to help teach him life lessons along the way. He wasn't proud that he hadn't graduated from high school but didn't let feelings of shame overtake him or keep him from learning. He was one of the most brilliant people that I have ever encountered. Brimming with street smarts and common sense, he loved learning by reading new things, watching news or documentaries, and exploring new places.

His curiosity was not limited to a finite number of subjects. He loved learning about various topics—technology, politics, history, leadership, sports, and medical technological developments were just a few that gained his attention. He absorbed material, and I was always impressed by his precise recall of information on such a vast array of subjects. His pursuit of knowledge was a gift to himself but to others as well, as it allowed him to connect with a variety of people and discuss their interests with intelligence and thoughtful care.

My dad taught me that learning "stuff" is not valuable unless you take the guidance and coaching of others to apply it. My dad reinforced the principle that if you are lucky enough for someone to take the time to coach or teach you, you should take it and run with it. In other words, it is your responsibility to react with coachability to the wisdom of others. Otherwise, you are wasting your own time and theirs.

My parents emphasized that education was paramount and that we were expected to learn and grow. They clearly outlined that our task was to pay attention in school and respect our teachers. Even if we disagreed with them, we were taught to respect their authority.

My dad's humble hungriness for knowledge was transferred to me, and no one was more proud of me than my dad when I walked across the stage to receive my degrees from Texas Tech and Cornell. Rick Collins may have been a high school dropout, but it was because of his example and coaching that I became an Ivy League graduate. He was my most valuable teacher in the lessons that mattered the most.

CHAPTER 13

Passion over Pain

*My dad lived in pain but did not live
a life of pain.*

In Vietnam, my father faced an unseen enemy whose constant attacks destroyed morale, leaving soldiers on edge and in a constant state of uneasy discomfort. When he returned home, a similar enemy met him in the form of chronic pain.

Chronic pain plagued my dad daily in an unrelenting onslaught, intent on terrorizing his spirit and endurance. Pain is like that. Whether physical or emotional, your brain screaming in pain is a powerful force of discouragement and a brutal enemy to face. It hurt my dad just to be. His pain was the gnawing, searing pain that tears at even the strongest individuals. It was exhausting for him to operate in such intense daily pain, yet he did. Just like in all things, he didn't shrink back—instead, he bravely ran to the fire of pain, acknowledging that it was part of his life and he had to choose to fight this battle well.

Armed with a wicked sense of humor and an immense love of football, my dad fought to endure his constant pain in nontraditional ways. My dad was uproariously funny, and he applied this humor to all aspects of his life in a manner that fit perfectly with his positive attitude mentality.

When informed that his cousin Ronnie, a fellow veteran, was returning years later to Vietnam post-war for a cathartic visit, my dad's humor was on full display.

"Rick, is there anything you want me to bring back from Vietnam for you?" Ronnie dutifully asked.

My dad quickly quipped, "Yes!"

Ronnie's eyebrows raised in expectation awaiting a solemn request.

"Please bring back my leg!" My dad declared as he and Ronnie burst into a chorus of raucous laughter.

My dad loved to laugh, and humor helped distract him from the intense nature of his injuries. It also made others around him more comfortable approaching him to ask questions.

My dad had a mischievous side to his humor that he especially employed when interacting with children who noticed he was missing a leg. One day, my dad was at an event and was not wearing his artificial leg. A little boy approached him and asked, "Where's your leg?"

My dad shrugged and replied, "I lost it." The answer seemed to satisfy the boy, who soon scampered off.

A few days later, my dad happened to be in the same location. This time, he was wearing his prosthetic leg.

The boy that had previously approached him happened to be there as well. He walked toward my dad with a bewildered look on his face.

"I thought you lost your leg," he queried.

"Well, lucky I found it," my dad replied teasingly.

My dad found humor to be therapeutic in the little things and the tough things, but coaching on the football field was where he truly found catharsis. Football was medicine to him, and his time on the field helped him to focus his attention outward instead of on the constant pain he was feeling.

Chronic pain, by nature, pulls your attention inward. *Why do I hurt so much? When will this pain stop? How can I function when everything hurts so much?* The feelings are valid and understandable, but they can easily turn into self-pity that erodes confidence and feelings of contribution.

My dad lived in pain but did not live a life of pain. It was vital to him that his pain had a purpose. After all that he endured, his experiences brought him to a place of choosing to live under pain and darkness or choosing to live in intentional positivity. As strange as it sounds, football became a platform for others to see everything that my dad modeled with daily intention. He set an evident example of a life lived differently. His family, friends, and the myriad children he coached throughout the decades could see that he lived life differently. This was a powerful witness to everyone that knew him.

Far from toxic positivity, my dad knew the reality of personal pain. He didn't diminish this reality, instead choosing to allow it to be a refining force that propelled his life forward.

The grass fields of the gridiron under the blazing Texas sun saw my dad leveraging football to take his mind off his own pain in pursuit of pushing others forward to achieve their best. With the aid of crutches, the labored gait of his twisting walk unmistakable on the sidelines, he was a fixture at football games for over fifty years. He would never hesitate to offer encouragement or insight to his players, wanting them to achieve their very best in all things.

Football was therapeutic for my father, and he recognized that it could be a tool to help heal others. His football playing years as a young man had taught him so much about channeling his fight and fire into something positive, and he worked diligently to help instill similar lessons in the children he coached. My dad gleaned as much information as possible from other prominent coaches to help enhance his coaching. He had learned a great deal from coaches that had encouraged him, disciplined him, and built confidence in him, and he felt that these mental models were intensely important to help mature young athletes.

Instead of focusing on his pain, he worked very hard to concentrate on producing young men of promise and character; football was the vehicle for these lessons.

A former player of my dad's, David Wray, once wrote me:

Chad, I wanted to tell you in a more personal way what your dad means to me. I remember hearing from a long distance other coaches yelling at their kids [players]. Your dad never did that. He truly coached us with patience and kindness. It was the right way to teach kids, and that was obvious from how we grew as players and a team. I took that lesson and apply it every day in how I treat employees. He truly taught us to be the kind of men we would strive to be. I wasn't smart enough to acknowledge it back then in my childhood, but I wanted you to know how important he is to me forty years later.

My dad was an incredible coach, but he uniquely saw beyond the football field. He knew he was helping raise other parents' children and strived to do that well. He set high standards for his players on and off the field and maintained higher standards for himself. No one could deny that my dad was tough. Anyone who gets knocked down and gets back up as often as he did is built with an inner resolve of steel, yet my dad maintained loving tenderness in how he handled people and as a coach.

A letter he once wrote to the editor of his local newspaper appropriately summed up the serious way he viewed his coaching and its impact:

Dear Editor, In response to the article "We Yell Because We Love Your Children," I would like the parents of Allen to know that, fortunately, the majority of coaches in ASA love your children enough NOT to yell. Condoning this type of verbal abuse in coaching, in my opinion, is irresponsible for any coach or board member.

Having served on the ASA board, I realize these types of incidents do occur and are overlooked by those who subscribe to the notion that "the coach is giving generously of his time and contributing to the community."

I vehemently disagree with this notion. These children also give freely of their time and energy. They come out to have fun and not be yelled and screamed at.

The duty of the coach is to instill confidence, not to tear it down with ranting and raving. A pat on the back and a word of encouragement do more to motivate a child to excel than a screaming coach ever will.

A closing note to those coaches who yell. The next time your employer screams and yells at you, tell me how that builds your character, self-confidence and motivates you to produce. Wouldn't a little recognition of your efforts go a lot further to achieve those goals?

A concerned coach and parent,
Rick Collins, Allen, Texas.

My dad poured his pain into constructive activities that served others. He never took out his pain on others or channeled it into things that further harmed him. He recognized that God had uniquely positioned him to be an example for others; this was not a role or responsibility he took lightly.

Another former player of my dad's and neighbor, Kevin Swint, wrote it this way:

I hope that he had some idea of how much he meant to me and how much impact he had on my life. If more people could have even one role model like him, the world would be a much better place. I can't think of anyone I've known who set a better example of how to live a noble life. I don't know where I'd be if I hadn't known him at a time when I so badly needed that example throughout my youth and teen years. He will always be the standard that I can try to live up to but never will. How lucky I am to have had him move in near me and coach and mentor me growing up. What a great man your father was.

My dad purposed his pain for God's glory, intentionally choosing to live a life of legacy that impacted all those around him. To this day, many people share with me that when they are struggling through pain or difficulty, they think of my dad and are inspired with hope, energy, fight, and conviction to change their attitude when addressing their challenges. The pain in my dad's life produced a powerful purpose as Rick chose to model gratitude, hope, and resiliency for others.

CHAPTER 14

F.A.M.I.L.Y.

**Loss had taught him that gain
requires investment.**

Sweat pebbled on the tip of my nose and along my hairline, threatening to drip down my face in tiny rivulets. I wiped it off with the back of my hand. I was baking in the summer heat, but that didn't dampen my desire to play on my imaginary front yard gridiron.

"Daddy! Daddy! Can you play with me?" I pleaded with my dad. "Can you throw the ball with me?"

It was over 100 degrees outside, and the sun was beating down in a brutalizing scorch. Most sensible adults hunkered down inside until the sun set and evening cool set in. My dad was not most men. He lived a motto of F.A.M.I.L.Y., which meant, "Forget about me; I love you." This wasn't a motto that meant his own needs weren't important. They were. This was a reminder that the time that we have with family is finite, and we need to make each moment count. He had learned this lesson the hard way with the loss of his first precious Linda and his son, Ricky Lynn.

Loss had taught him that gain requires investment. So whenever I asked for help or his time, he made sure that he was there. Even with temperatures in the triple digits and battling intense pain, he wouldn't hesitate to teach me football, basketball, baseball, or whatever game I was begging him to learn. He knew that time was valuable, and he wanted to spend it well.

His investment in me was not without cost to himself. Often, I would watch him return to the house after playing with me in the yard to see him removing his unwieldy plaster prosthetic. He would peel off the sock that covered the stump of his leg and reveal raw, red skin that was often cracked and bleeding or covered in oozing blisters. He didn't say "no" when 99 percent of other people would have, because he recognized that no matter how painful, his investment in me and others would pay off in dividends.

Giving freely of his time and love fueled my dad. No matter the pain or the wear and tear of getting to and from the stadium or basketball court, my dad never missed a game. He was there for my sister and me, and when we had our own children, he multiplied his efforts to make sure that he was always present for his four grandchildren. One constant that secured us all was that my dad was always there to provide a positive smile, encouraging words, or a mammoth-sized bear hug. The knowledge that he would always be there for us impacted us all.

When he spoke the words, "I love you," they were an invaluable currency, as they were backed by the gold of a lived standard. He showed us that *I love you* was more action than words. It was a verb that, when lived, meant empathy for others, comfort, and connection. This spurred us to live lives full of richness.

My dad instructed us that life is too short and tomorrow is never promised, so he tried to live as fully as possible. He faced constant setbacks, endless surgeries, and unending chronic pain. When I was growing up, I was always worried that these challenges would cost him his life at an age far too young. I tried to prepare myself for what I feared was inevitable. My sister, Caryn, did as well. She worried that my dad would never live to see her married or walk her down the aisle.

Those with chronic pain often have a decreased life expectancy, and this was made more complex than the extreme nature of Rick's devastating injuries. My dad persisted, though. He gave my sister away at her wedding and was there when each of his grandchildren was born. I am certain that Rick Collins lived longer because he lived better. He loved us fiercely, and this gave him the fight to keep going.

His family received the firstfruits of his love, but this never left him lacking of love to give. My dad extended his F.A.M.I.L.Y. policy to friends and neighbors as well. In his heart, they were family. He would sit and talk or listen to friends for hours. He made them all feel as if they mattered. When someone shared something tough, he was empathetic and encouraging. If someone shared something exciting, he rejoiced in celebration. He was the first to cheer anyone on. He lived in the moment, always thinking of others instead of focusing on his own hardships.

Amazingly, his action-filled love even extended to his beloved dogs. He had two dogs for many years, and he always told them that he loved them. One of them was a sweet dachshund named Kippy. Kippy was accidentally run over by a car. Literally split in two, his organs oozed from his body. He was rushed to the emergency room, where the vet cautioned my dad that it was unlikely that Kippy would live.

My dad knew that the odds against him meant that there were odds to overcome, so he told the vet to do whatever was needed to save his dog. Weeks went by, accompanied by a series of surgeries. Kippy was still alive, but it was touch and go. My dad would not give up if anything could be done to save Kippy.

Months passed, and the vet bill climbed to over thirty thousand dollars, but my dad never gave up. Kippy eventually pulled through, making a full recovery. I am quite sure that Kippy had no idea how lucky he was to have Rick Collins as an owner, but loving someone so much that he wouldn't give up on him was the standard operating procedure for my dad.

This love produced a richness of family, unlike anything that most people will ever know. Monetarily, we didn't have much, but my dad always made his pension stretch to anything that we needed. The wealth of our family didn't lie in financial means; it was measured in moments of love.

Our home was rich in love, respect, patriotism, gratefulness, and service to others because of my dad's faithful and consistent investment in the things that mattered most. He gave without ever expecting a return, yet he knew that the investment would multiply, allowing generations to flourish from his legacy.

My dad's example and time poured into us yielded huge returns. I always felt like the luckiest son in the world to have a dad who always wanted me around. When I was still a toddler, he took me with him to the gym as well as to all the practices and games of the teams that he coached. This never felt like a burden to him or me; it gave me an innate sense of belonging. I was so proud to be with my dad. He may have walked stiffly and slowly and been covered in a roadmap of scars, but none of that bothered me or caused me self-consciousness. What mattered is that my dad wanted to spend his time with me.

My dad was always pouring into me and going above and beyond to serve those around him. I didn't fully grasp how unusual this was until I started spending time with friends and watching their inter-actions with their parents. If I went to a friend's house to sleep over or went out and came back late, other parents were usually sleeping by the time we got in.

This was not the case for my dad. He made it a priority to wait up at night and make sure that we were home safe at curfew. He always said, "I love you" at the end of the night. He wanted to ensure that we went to bed each day knowing that we were safe and loved.

Each morning, my dad made sure that we were greeted with a smile. He emphasized the importance of "Do unto others as you would have them do unto you." His model of this was measured in the lessons that we learned through his love.

Forget about me; I love you.

CHAPTER 15

I Got You

**The only thing that can
hold you back is you.**

I gripped my dad tightly as his steady swimming stroke sliced through the shimmering aquamarine water of the hotel pool. Family vacations, whether to the mountains or the beach, always included a pool. The hotel was usually a modest family budget stay, but my dad always insisted that it had to have a pool.

"Just hold your breath and hold on to me; I got you," my dad instructed.

He would swim Caryn or me to the deep end while we clung tightly to our dad. His words calmed us and gave us confidence; we were never scared to step out of our comfort zone when bolstered by the loving support of our dad.

"I got you." These three simple words overflowed with endless meaning.

These words from my dad showed me that it was okay to try difficult things, that I could push myself past uncomfortable limits and know that my dad would always be there for me.

Dad would chide, "The only thing that can hold you back is you." He wanted both Caryn and me to push ourselves to overcome hard things so that we would see that limits are there only if we let them be.

I burned to be everything that my dad thought I could be and more than even he could imagine. I pushed myself to excel in sports and academics, not because of pressure from my parents but because of the pride in my name: Collins.

I wanted to show others the legacy that my dad had left on me. He had forged the Collins identity, but it was my turn to take the torch and keep it blazing.

Of course, not to be outdone, my dad was still running the race. He encouraged the positive annihilating of perceived limits, and he also did just that.

The only thing that can hold you back is you. I am sure these words echoed in Rick's head day after day as he summoned the strength to get back up each time that pain or life knocked him down. He didn't let his disabilities or amputation keep him from gathering as many life experiences as possible.

Rick Collins was always up for a challenge or to try something new. This was not limited to riding his Harley-Davidson Trike motorcycle all around the country with close friends John Spencer, Steve Beagle, and Keith Weinman, although that was a feat. He also ventured on a horse in the mountains of New Mexico, rode wave runners at the lake, and drove snowmobiles in Oregon and Colorado. He was not a conservative rider either; he went full force ahead. Occasionally, this meant turning over snowmobiles, which I am not sure thrilled my mom, especially when she was his passenger on two of these snowmobile spills. My dad was always willing to try something new, even if it was difficult.

He was such a great role model to watch, especially when he was such a strong advocate through his affirming words to me. I looked to emulate him by daring greatly and pushing beyond limits.

The Collins family pride accompanied me to Allen High School in Allen, Texas, where I was a four-sport athlete. There, my passion was undeniably football, which was undoubtedly influenced by my dad's love of the sport. There, I gravitated to the position of quarterback due to the leadership qualities that my dad had honed in me as I was growing up. A quarterback must stay cool in the face of adversity, not getting rattled or discouraged if the game gets behind. He must stay positive and radiate that energy to his teammates, recognizing that in even the bleakest of circumstances, there's always a chance to rally and win. These are qualities that my dad instilled in me from childhood.

Even with no chance of a miracle, the passion to go down trying was what set the bar for me. My dad never went down without a fight, reminding me, "Collinses will never quit." Fighting forward instead of folding was ingrained in the culture of my family and was on full display every time I stepped foot on that field. I would fight like hell to make sure that I left it all on the field, and then get up and do it again the very next game.

If I am being completely candid, I have to admit that I wasn't the most gifted quarterback, but I fought to be. Thankfully, I was decent enough to get some college offers, including an appointment and opportunity to play at West Point, the United States Military Academy.

Verbally committed and ready to sign in February of 1992, I woke up the day before signing with an uneasy feeling. Maybe it was like my dad's disconcerting premonition in Vietnam—I don't really know. I just knew that sometimes the boldest thing that you can do is change course, and I needed to change direction.

As appealing as playing at West Point was, I knew that I needed peace in this monumental decision. I also recognized that the needed reassurance of my dad's "I got you" would be more difficult if I went to a school that was far away. Flying was difficult due to my dad's stiff leg, and I knew that it would be hard if he had to miss out on my games. I was ready to stretch past limits, but I wasn't quite at the place of leaping out of my dad's safe arms.

I remember calling Coach Denny Doornbos and Coach Bob Sutton and sharing my gratefulness for their opportunity and explaining that God had a different path for me. That gave me peace.

After a flurry of calls to football programs that had previously offered but had since moved on, I chose a more difficult path. I decided to become a walk-on at Texas Tech University in the hope of earning the opportunity to play under coach Spike Dykes.

Schools have an investment in scholarship players. This is not the case for walk-ons, who have to fight and push to prove their worth. As a quarterback in high school, I had to apply myself fully to learning a new position as I fought for a spot in my new role as a safety.

I loved playing at Texas Tech. It was a great experience, and I was surrounded by amazing teammates. However, my college career didn't end up being quite what I envisioned for myself. I had a nagging shoulder injury that I tried to play through, ultimately to my own detriment. I tried to fight through it for years. Finally, I realized that my time as a collegiate football player had come to an end when the surgeon determined that I needed major surgery and would have to sit out a full year to rehabilitate my shoulder.

I called my parents, bawling. After all of my hard work, I didn't want to retire from football but knew that I needed to. On the phone, my dad did exactly what he always had done. He uplifted me, encouraging me that the brightest part of my future was yet to unfold. He expressed how proud he was of me and encouraged me to continue striving for more in life. He reminded me that I controlled my future through attitude, effort, and coachability while instructing me to always be the best teammate to others. These attributes that he had instilled in me since childhood are the same characteristics that I successfully apply to business and all other endeavors to this day.

With my time on the football field ending, my dad encouraged me to go after new things and not fear failure in trying. I pivoted quickly, working to grow as a business and community leader during my remaining time at Texas Tech and beyond. I was elected senator on the Texas Tech Student Senate, became vice president of the Texas Tech Student Alumni Board, and served as a member of the College of Business President's Leadership Council. I turned my passion for being part of a team in a new direction while learning and growing along the way.

After graduating with a degree in business, I married my childhood friend, Kelly Beagle. An elementary school teacher and school counselor, she is a brilliant complement to my life. We began to build our life together in Dallas, Texas, not too far from where my dad had grown up. I was hired by American Greetings, a large greeting card company, where I worked for two years while I tried to line up the opportunities that I wanted to establish for long-term growth.

After everything that my dad had gone through medically, I was extremely interested in pursuing a job in the field of healthcare. Finally, I got the call that I had been waiting for. Sanofi Pharmaceuticals offered me the opportunity to build a global health-care career. Throughout my career, through hard work and blessing, I have been fortunate to be involved with Sanofi Pharmaceuticals, a top five global pharmaceutical company; Stryker, one of the most well-known medical device companies; and Galderma, the largest global dermatology company.

Through my roles, I have been able to lead thousands of employees and travel the world. This led to where I am now. I co-founded and currently serve as the CEO and chairman of the board of my own healthcare company called Corganics (www.corganics. com). Corganics' sole purpose is to help patients in need who are struggling with pain or health and wellness issues. Watching my dad's fight with pain for all those years gave me the purpose of pursuing options to help better care for those challenged by pain and physical problems.

Inspired by my dad, this career has provided many opportunities for my family that we are grateful for. Kelly and I are blessed to have three incredible children, Carson, Chief, and Caroline. I am so proud of each of my children and know that my dad would be as well. He loved them so much.

My sister Caryn and husband Matt Moore have a son named Lucas. All four of my dad's grandchildren were a rich blessing to him. His imprint is seen in each of them. They all beam with big Rick Collins smiles, approaching life with genuine joy in their hearts. They put others first, which makes them loving and loyal friends. They have an uncanny maturity when it comes to showing empathy for others. They love spending time with family and carry on the Collins passion for sports, competition, and teamwork.

My dad instilled a legacy in me but also in them. All three of my children work extremely hard and excel academically and athletically, which I know is due to my dad's constant support of them in whatever endeavors they chose to pursue. He would be proud to know that Carson is now a quarterback at the University of Tulsa and about to graduate, Chief plays safety at Texas Tech University, and Caroline plays volleyball at one of the top vollyball programs in the country. Coach Collins imparted the foundations for these achievements.

I got you.

My dad's reassurance extended to his grandkids. Their proud "Papa," he never missed their football games, and growing up, they reveled in this, looking forward to post-game conversations with him, discussing plays and tactics for improving before their next game. They always knew that my dad was invested in supporting them, no matter what.

Not without their own share of football injuries, Carson and Chief always looked to Papa as an example of how to fight forward through hardship.

In his junior year, Carson dislocated his knee, resulting in a torn medial patellofemoral ligament, torn cartilage, and chipped bone, but he refused to sit a season out with reconstructive surgery. He waited until the season was over and had the surgery in the off-season, returning to the game he loved, taped up and prepared to keep playing. Each week he would have to drain his knee, icing and rehabbing hard to be able to play. After all, "Collinses will never quit." Carson reflected often that Papa was his inspiration to know that he could handle anything in his path. Carson enjoyed another playoff season his senior year before earning his opportunity to play in college.

Chief also was lured by the Collins family siren call of the football field. His junior year of high school, as a starting wide receiver and safety, he dove after the ball a few moments before the clock ran out. When he picked himself up from the fray, he was gripping his shoulder; his collarbone had snapped. The team's orthopedic surgeon advised that a complete break meant he would be out for the entire season. Summoning his Collins strength, Chief asked, "Can I have surgery?" He wanted to determine if undergoing the knife would allow him the chance to come back that season.

The surgeon reluctantly replied, "Yes," and two days later, Chief underwent surgery that allowed him to get back to the field a mere six weeks later. He worked hard to stay in shape while resting and rehabbing his shoulder, and it mended in time for him to be able to play the remaining season and playoff games without incident. This built great momentum into his senior season, where he was awarded First Team All-state after recording seven interceptions with three returned for touchdowns, propelling him to college football offers.

When I look at my boys, I see my dad's fighting spirit and love for others shine through them. What an incredible legacy he left. Caroline and Lucas carry it too—a beautiful balance of toughness and tenderness.

My dad's dedication to serve others was a major force in my own life, providing me with incredible inspiration to do the same. I wanted to take up the mantle that he wore so well. Over the years, I have coached hundreds of youth in various sports, although, like my dad, my passion for football pulled me in that direction.

My dad's devotion to coaching taught me to be a great player and a loving coach. His passion for learning and education was also an investment. He fought for others to succeed in that. My dad did not graduate from high school, yet he coached me to value education, which was evidenced when I had the privilege of graduating with my MBA from Cornell, an Ivy League university.

My dad always gave me the opportunity to build on the firm Collins foundation that he had started. I grew my educational opportunities, expanded my business ventures, coached, and devoted myself to supporting the education of others in the same way that my dad supported me. This led to me spending twelve years serving on the Lovejoy ISD School Board as an officer and in the role of president. I found joy in serving others. Like my dad, I recognized our youth deserve a great education, and it was an honor to serve in this role for many years.

My dad was instrumental in helping me understand how to balance life—competing in business at the highest levels, developing and mentoring others personally and professionally, serving my community, coaching kids, and most of all, loving my family and friends with all my heart.

My dad's impact on me is felt every day as I take his life lessons to heart. While I have been blessed immensely with my own family, career, and opportunities, I, too, face challenges and fires that test my will to persevere. It is in these moments that I sit in silence and hear my dad's whisper echo in my heart.

I got you.

EPILOGUE

What's Your Christmas?

**May you be the kind of person who would
live boldly and run to the fire.**

Christmas was my dad's favorite holiday. He lit up brighter than the twinkling lights on a Christmas tree when the holiday season came around. He gleefully celebrated the presents, the laughter, and especially the cherished time with his family.

My dad brimmed with a childlike enthusiasm for everything Christmas. Maybe it was because of that terrible Christmas in Vietnam when, instead of seeing Bob Hope's Christmas special, he trembled in terror as he confronted the enemy of fear, or maybe it was because he recognized that life was truly a gift. Either way, my dad made every moment of Christmas count.

Often tight on money, my dad scrimped and saved, sacrificing to go all out on our Christmas gifts. We were never disappointed as Caryn and I danced with delight at the sight of our family Christmas tree packed with presents.

Rick's holiday generosity poured past his family and into the lives of others. No one was in need on his watch. Strangers became family and were welcomed into our house for the holidays. Those struggling to afford gifts or going without left our house with arms full and hearts uplifted. My dad knew how to care for others. This was his Christmas. He made it his mission to care for everyone that God gathered into his life.

My dad's sacrificial love for people was matched only by the strength of his convictions. This was demonstrated every day, and the Christmas season was no exception. One year, a prominent big-box retailer determined not to allow its employees to say, "Merry Christmas," and it enacted a new policy that prohibited the Salvation Army from ringing their bells in front of these stores.

My dad felt convicted to act. He believed that these policies were wrong, and he was determined to fight against them. He showed up to protest.

Day one: He protested alone, standing outside of the store for hours on his increasingly uncomfortable prosthetic.

Day two: He was still there. No one else ran to the fire to join him in the fight against something he considered to be wrong.

Day three: He remained. Steadfast in his conviction, people were beginning to take note. Within a few days, he was surrounded by supporters. Others joined in and stood by him as he peacefully stood up for what he believed in.

He protested for three weeks, gaining momentum, visibility, and a crowd of supporters. Eventually, the news got wind of it and featured the story. The moral conviction of Rick Collins created a movement that gained enough traction to cause the nationwide chain to change its stance. In typical Rick Collins style, he didn't quit, and his persistence changed the world around him.

What is your Christmas? What is the thing that calls to you, inspiring you to run toward the fire to make a lasting difference in the lives that you influence? To my dad, Christmas was a literal and figurative representation of something that lifts your spirit and pours into it, a purpose that fills you even as you pour out to others.

My dad's "Christmas" went far beyond the lights and delights of his celebrating children and grandchildren. It was even greater than the coaching or causes that he poured himself out for.

Rick Collins' core purpose, drive, and reason for living an extraordinary life came from his personal relationship with Jesus Christ. This was the driving force behind everything that he did, every sacrifice that he made, and every kindness that he overflowed with toward others.

His relationship with his Lord and Savior gave him the strength to live an immeasurable life of intentional impact that resonated with everyone fortunate enough to know him.

My dad's relationship with the Lord was at the heart of absolutely everything that he did. This was the legacy that he passed down to our family. This is the light that guides us in his absence.

Richard Frank Collins passed away on December 19, 2020, at the age of seventy-one. His loss was heaven's gain, and I know without a doubt that he was greeted by the words written in Matthew 25:23 (ESV): *"Well done, good and faithful servant. You have been faithful over a little; I will set you over much. Enter into the joy of your master."*

Rick Collins left behind an enduring legacy of love. It is my hope that in reading this book, you have been touched by his story and inspired to live a life of intention, regardless of your circumstances. May you be the kind of person who would live boldly and run to the fire.

A Note from the Author

Rick Collins is not the only incredible hero among us. Many have faced incredible odds and persevered. I sincerely hope that this book will help others bring those stories to light so that we can celebrate them. My dad instilled in me intense admiration for our combat military veterans, law enforcement, and first responders who put their lives on the line to serve others. It is my hope that we can bring light to other stories like my dad's where we can highlight those brave, courageous men and women that face difficult journeys but find a way to get up and run to the fire in their own unique ways. We look forward to hearing your story at www.runtothefire.me.

Rick Collins

Dad in Vietnam

Christmas

Mom and Dad

Dad coaching

Dad and family at football game

Dad and family in early family photo

Dad

Chad and Dad at Vietnam Memorial Wall

www.ingramcontent.com/pod-product-compliance
Lightning Source LLC
Chambersburg PA
CBHW030503100426
42813CB00002B/317